LEAP YEAR

LEAP YEAR

A Year in the Life of a Dancer

Christopher d'Amboise

FOREWORD BY LINCOLN KIRSTEIN
PHOTOGRAPHS BY CAROLYN GEORGE

DOUBLEDAY & COMPANY, INC.
GARDEN CITY, NEW YORK
1982

ACKNOWLEDGMENTS

Without the constant aid, far beyond duty's call, of Richard Boehm, this book would probably have buried me.

With great respect, I thank the close friends of the d'Amboises whose invaluable support strengthened me.

Thank you, Manuela, for the most timely assistance.

I am grateful to Sally Arteseros for all her talents, effort, and enthusiasm.

Special gratitude to Mrs. Jacqueline Onassis who supported me, encouraged me, and helped me form this book.

PERMISSIONS

Terence This Is Stupid Stuff by A. E. Houseman
Copyright © 1965 by Holt, Rinehart & Winston. Reprinted by permission of the publisher.

"BOOGIE WOOGIE BUGLE BOY"
Words and Music by DON RAYE and HUGHIE PRINCE
© Copyright 1940, 1941 by MCA MUSIC, A DIVISION OF MCA INC., New York, N. Y. Copyright renewed. USED BY PERMISSION
ALL RIGHTS RESERVED

DESIGNED BY LAURENCE ALEXANDER

Library of Congress Catalog Card Number 82-45352
ISBN: *0-385-17449-7*
Copyright © 1982 by Christopher d'Amboise

With great admiration to Carolyn & Jacques,
better known as Mom and Dad

FOREWORD

Christopher d'Amboise is the son of two exceptionally brilliant dancers. Jacques, his father, still dances, and perhaps more importantly invents ballets and teaches hundreds of boys, if not how to dance, at the least, what ballet can promise. Carolyn George, his mother, had a leap like a man, but with it, the strength and sweetness of an accomplished ballerina. Chris was born with precious spoons in his mouth. If it did not make it easier for him to be an excellent academic dancer, because this is easy for no one whatever their provenance, it gave him the luck not to spend vital energy, physical and metaphysical, fighting his family.

Not twenty years ago I listened to an anguished daddy plead with me not to encourage his very gifted pride and joy to persist in the folly of becoming a classic dancer. A well-meaning stockbroker, he saw a career in the ballet as pure perdition. "I'd rather see that boy dead, than *dance!*" The child didn't dance; perhaps Wall Street won another victory. But, somehow, over the last two decades, Apollo and Terpsichore have won; now preadolescent males can go to class every day, and appear a couple of times a week in George Balanchine's and Jerry Robbins' repertory at the State Theater in Lincoln Center.

The emergence of Christopher, and of growing bands of companions, marks a real change of heart and mind. The male principle in ballet has been restored where it's belonged, for centuries, after a disastrous interval when the greed of management exploited nineteenth-century ballerinas, friends and enemies of Taglioni and Elssler, as negotiable securities. The role of male partners was reduced to anonymous support, to such a degree that girls, *en travesti,* took their place, which gave male dancers a bad name. The male criterion never died; we who never saw him invoke the name of Nijinsky as our patron and paragon.

Today we can read that certain giant basketball players have the grace of a dancer. Twenty years ago it was placatory praise to say that a dancer had the force of an athlete. Jacques d'Amboise and Eddie Villela cleared the path for us, and it was broadened by Rudolph Nureyev and Mikhail Baryshnikov. Today, in our schools, little boys can imagine themselves without social anxiety as performing artists. The fact that this transformation is almost presupposed shows the strength and depth of a wonderful mutation.

Although Chris was to the manner born, and could judge the quality of a dancer's skill with his Cornflakes, he inherited also the rare capacity to surpass instinct and blind muscular energy. One could say he's a bright boy; too often brightness is a mere concomitant of youthful muscle; it dulls with maturity. As readers of this extraordinary book will find, brightness here means brain; his whole book is a metaphor for the presence of analytical judgment. Some dancers behave in life, as well as on the stage, as hypnotized somnambulists, who never need to wake, since their training serves as a substitute for a psychic spine. There is a common error that the unconscious artist, a magically gifted "primitive," is happier than those awake enough to realize who and what they are. But it is not these, however brilliant they become, who continue the dynasty and destiny of ballet. They have their service and satisfaction, but it is different in kind and longevity from the relatively unhappy few who are both fine performers and thinking analysts.

Christopher writes close to the bone. He is not a victim of romantic balletomania. Every dancer who risks the extremity of muscle is in hazard. It's hard to learn how not to get hurt—the difference between fatigue and bad judgment. It's not easy to make cold and even ungenerous judgment of choreography to which one is assigned or committed. It is almost impossible to suspend natural cravings in the self and not grant despair fifty-one percent of one's effort. I know of no other account written by a dancer that puts the physical and metaphysical in useful order. Chris doesn't teach, yet. Fortunately he has twenty years ahead in which he doesn't have to. He may not surpass his parents as soloists in their comparative context, but there's every sign he'll extend their important service.

The author of this book has a neat literary style. "Neat" is a word that in current jargon means more than "tidy." Elegance, economy, and laconic judgment have given Chris a big jump, elevation, or leap. He's a cheerful character, and his careful thought should bring cheer to generations of aspirants to the great tradition he honors.

LINCOLN KIRSTEIN
May 4, 1982

PREFACE

"I knew the instant I first saw a ballet that I had to become a dancer." I have heard other dancers make such a proclamation in explanation of why they dance.

I never said anything like that.

My father is a dancer, my mother was a dancer, my aunt and uncle were dancers, my brother and two sisters all took ballet lessons. Ballet was as fundamental a part of our lives as brushing our teeth. I do not recall with any vividness my first meal upon this earth or the first time I brushed my teeth. Neither do I remember my first exposure to dance. Of the four children, I was the only to follow ballet as a profession. Why? Perhaps for the same reason that I had the fewest cavities—I brushed more often. I stuck with the ballet when the others had discarded it. I admit this is not a very obsessive account of one's reasons for dancing, but I was not obsessive. It was fun. That's all; like playing basketball was fun.

Most of the actions I undertook as a child I never bothered to question. I assumed that there was a practical reason for all of them. Consequently, I became a professional dancer without really knowing what I was in for. Of course I knew about the field, but I knew all the answers without ever having asked the questions.

At age eighteen I followed the path of my aunt, uncle, father and mother and joined New York City Ballet. I was as familiar with the company as if it were an extension of my family. I was confident of my ability to fit right in. However, life within the company proved to be a great deal more turbulent than I had anticipated. I was confronted with all the questions I had never asked. It was a surprise that I found myself feeling guilt-ridden, excessive, perverse, often ecstatic, often miserable, and most importantly, obsessive!

Everyone allows the young to ask all the wrong questions, as well as the right ones. Everyone understands a boy's extensive and excessive search for something directly under his nose, or for something he could never find. Youth can justify the most outlandish opinions. How wonderful to have opinions. They are the strength of our character. The best thing about them is that there is no disproving them; there are no incorrect opinions. Not only that, but you can change them whenever you want!

APRIL

The d'Amboise family 1968.

As long as I can remember John Taras has been a company ballet master. He often wears the same gold-studded belt and blue jeans, which is uncharacteristic for he is basically a sincere and conservative man.

On Saturday morning John Taras was teaching class. Halfway through the class, halfway through the *adagio*, halfway through the *promenade* in *à la seconde,* my leg cramped. Well not really a bad cramp but holding the leg extended to the side and revolving slowly did not produce agreeable sensations. I leaped at any ploy to quit the combination, and playing up a minor cramp proved sufficient. I glanced out of the corner of my eye to see if my father had noticed. He was working intensely on the other side of the studio and was temporarily unaware of me. Although Balanchine had given me permission to take his company's class, I only came when my father was there also, otherwise I was fearfully intimidated by the large studio filled with professional dancers. I was not in the company. It was my eleventh year as a student in the School of American Ballet, the exclusive school to NYCB. When I did not attend the company class I was at the school, where classes were more comfortable for me.

Dropping the leg I dramatically rubbed the thigh while limping to the side of the studio. Suddenly a curious sensation swept through the studio, a stifling, stiffening tremor. Everyone seemed affected. Conversation stopped and people, previously standing leisurely on the side, busied themselves. What had caused this curious metamorphosis? I worried that perhaps my feigned cramp had been noticed. I continued to entertain this absurd notion until seeing the real reason standing in the shadow of the back door:

BALANCHINE!

I wondered if he had seen me stop halfway through the combination. No, if he even noticed me at all, he probably wondered what I was doing there. Did he remember he had given me permission?

Despite his presence, the class continued unfalteringly, everyone pretending to be unaware of him. The next step was a jumping combination. I rejoined the group. Now Mr. B. would see something greater than a pitiful *promenade* in *à la seconde!* I fitted my feet into fifth position and leaped high into the air. Out of the corner of my eye I glanced into the mirror to see if he was watching me. He was gone! The doorway was empty.

The cramp returned to my leg and I limped to the side again.

With five minutes left in class, I noticed the prolonged absence of my father. He had gone out into the hall, I assumed for a drink of water, but he had not returned. Even though age and mileage had reduced much of his elevation, he never missed the jumps. Immediately after I discovered his absence the door burst open and he came bounding into the room heading straight for me, suppressing a grin. He threw his arms around me. He often showed this kind of affection, yet I wondered what had warranted this sudden outburst. He whispered in my ear:

"Congratulations, you just got into the New York City Ballet!"

His words stunned me, "What?" I asked tentatively, fearing I had misunderstood.

"I went out into the hall for a drink of water," he explained. "Mr. B. was out there. He had seen you in class and he said, 'I think it is time Chris joined. He is ready.' "

"Really?" I was tingling with excitement. The exhilaration was almost enough to completely cloud my reasoning, but through it I managed a practical thought:

"But I have two more months of high school!"

"Oh." My father stopped. "Well, when do you finish?"

"June."

"Oh," he repeated.

We stood, both bewildered, for some time.

"Wait!" I said. "I can do a senior project!"

"What's that?"

"Don't worry, I'll be out of school in a week!"

I hugged him again and we did the jumps together.

At the Collegiate School for Boys, after completing all academic requirements, a senior has the option of engaging in an outside project of his choice. If the school judges this "senior project" worthy of credit, then the student need not attend the last semester of school at all. His only requirements are to successfully fulfill his project and to be present at graduation. My senior project was joining the New York City Ballet. Never had Collegiate received such a proposal. After some hesitation the school agreed that this was indeed worthy of credit. So the end of my school life coincided with the start of a professional one. I can hardly describe the excitement I felt. No more exams! Never again would the alarm clock buzz at 7:30 A.M.! No more guilt over insufficiently prepared homework! I believed all these things to be behind me, and happy days were clearly in sight!

I felt it very valuable to complete high school, yet I was thrilled to carry home my last load of books knowing it was finished. From now on I would be carrying dirty dance clothes instead.

It is rare for a dancer to attain a formal education. Obsessively driven dancers, particularly girls, reach heights of drive and dedication at very young ages. With skinny bodies and bright eyes these girls plunge into the life of dance. They think of little else; other things don't interest them. School becomes a nuisance, a constant itch piquing for attention. Some give up school altogether, to the dismay of their parents. A common alternative is the correspondence course by which the student receives homework and exams through the mail. It is a quick and easier path to a diploma. The parents are assuaged, and the scholastic itch is minor. However, a frequent result of insufficient education is a tall slim woman with bright eyes who doesn't know or care about anything but dance. So ballet dancers have gained the reputation of being unable to hold a conversation about anything but their *pointe* shoes. This is not due to a lack of intelligence, but merely to a lack of diversified interests. All their skill, imagination, and desire are so keenly focused, that like horses with blinders they see just one path before them.

I now travel along the same path but feel only partially blinded. There is a flaw in my blinders enabling me to spy several possible detours. I see the path as a large country road flanked on either side by occasional dwellings. Each abode holds a different enticement, each promises warmth and discovery. There is a little one-story oak cottage, congested with dusty books, where I might sit alone and explore each page of every volume. There is a large elegant dacha that offers inexhaustible orchestras that play glorious classical music, which I could learn about. There is an English clubhouse where in heavy chairs and a smoky atmosphere men sit sipping port and discussing philosophy, with pipes dangling from their mouths as they speak. Each of these enclosures attracts me, but if I deviate from the road to investigate, I might fall behind the others who did not stray. Who is better off? To indulge these outside interests, encouraging them to flourish, might very well retard a dancer's progress. But I don't think I can give up anything; I want everything.

My early attempts to combine ballet with academia resulted in an onerous half alliance to both, with me belonging absolutely to neither. In the tenth grade, an anxiety arose to vex the students—"college." To many of my classmates, college was an essential concern. I could not understand this. As far as I cared, school was a burden to be jettisoned. However, my friends' apprehension sparked a previously quiescent flicker of question within me. I had never designed my future any farther than a summer vacation. So, I then posed to myself the question that all students must, "What do you want to do with your life?" I always adored basketball, but had the sense to realize that I was neither seven feet tall nor black. So the Knicks were out. I have always found that problems are easier to resolve when I mentally picture them. So I applied this to aid in the resolution of my question. I could produce no image at all of a sports-oriented life. A dim, unvaried picture of college appeared. However, the vision of dancing was shining and noble! I suppose there was never really any doubt; merely a want of realization.

With this new assurance of mind, I felt an unfamiliar sense of relief and excitement. So in the tenth grade I resigned from the basketball team and devoted all after-school time to dancing. My parents and I were in mutual agreement that although college was not a necessity, a high school diploma was important.

"But what do you want to do when you finish dancing?" the parents of my school friends demanded, unable to comprehend the value of a career in which a mandatory retirement followed middle age. They felt that one should direct one's youth toward work that brought security. "Even if the work is distasteful, suffer young so that at middle age you have financial security, and any desires may then be pursued."

The dancer views life in the opposite light. One must fulfill one's desires now, be happy now, harbor no anxieties about the future. Indulge in the pleasure available to youth. Trust that when the dancing must end there will be other desires awaiting acknowledgment. Neither philosophy can be deemed superior, but I do believe that all joys and sorrows reach their height of intensity while in youth. All things should be experienced at the peak of ripeness.

All schoolbooks I placed neatly on the shelf. Several of them had never been opened, but now, as a result of their newly diminished importance, they looked interesting. School was over forever. At eighteen, I was a full-time member of the *corps de ballet* in the New York City Ballet. My father, who started professionally at fifteen, became a principal dancer at eighteen and was now forty-four.

People often tell me how horrible it must be to dance in the same company as one's famous father. They advise, with pity in their voices, that I must not boil with jealousy and should learn to be my own person. I believe them. After all, they are grown-ups and must know what they are talking about. Only I don't feel what they describe. To me my father is a friend, a mentor even, not a father. I hold few childhood memories of him. He was dancing so incessantly that neither my sisters, my brother, nor I saw much of him. We would be asleep when he returned late at night and off to school before he awakened. Occasionally, he appeared for dinner. He would be tired, often irritable, and sometimes terrifying. However, as I grew up and started dancing more and more, he grew up and danced less and less. Thus, our paths crossed more frequently. His fierceness quickly eroded, washed away by his new-found amiability. So now, as two friends we work together, laugh together, talk about women and sex. I sometimes take liberties with him that most parents would scorn as disrespectful of a son to a father—but not of a friend to a friend. I feel guilty about not having the heated jealousy toward him that people claim I must. I have failed somehow, for there are things about my father that one could take offense with. But since I like him as much as I feel filial affection, I must conclude that my inadequate jealousy is due to a fault in me.

Since Collegiate is an all-boys' school, derogatory remarks about homosexuality were frequent. As the only ballet dancer, I received more than my share. In the tenth grade a drastic change occurred. It was announced that

Jacques d'Amboise would be giving a dance demonstration on Thursday afternoon. A few of my classmates knew the tall, sharp man who is my father. Others had heard of him from their parents. And the rest must have been just curious. For whatever reason, the gymnasium was packed with students in loose-fitting jackets and ties (such is the Collegiate dress code). On viewing the immense crowd one might suppose a basketball championship was to be played. Sitting in the corner of the gym was the head of the athletic department, his features twisted with concern about the basketball court, which my father had covered with Comet cleanser to prevent slipping. My father stood near, reassuring him that there would be no damage to the floor. Elise, a young ballerina from the company, would be dancing also. I was extremely nervous. My father was wearing a pink leotard and black tights. I worried that his choice of color was not particularly masculine. Elise, however, was in a white leotard and tights. She wore a chiffon skirt around her waist. She wasn't wearing a bra and looked very sexy. This was a consolation. I figured that my classmates would be too busy gaping at Elise to notice the color of my father's leotard.

Jacques walked onto the middle of the gym and addressed the boys. He has always been dexterous with an audience, and proved so again, by immediately introducing Elise, who received tremendous applause and whistles. They danced "The Man I Love" *pas de deux* from Balanchine's ballet *Who Cares.* They performed beautifully despite the bad conditions. When they finished the boys applauded warmly, but I didn't feel that they were particularly impressed.

While the performers were catching their breath, a boy in the audience made a remark. I couldn't hear what he had said, but I'm sure it pertained to Elise. Whatever was said must have been funny, for almost every jacket and tie in the gym started bouncing with laughter. This caught my father's attention.

"What's so funny?" he scowled. "Do you think all this dancing is easy?" The boys stiffened in silence. My father continued, "Well, it's a lot harder than you think. Now watch!" He took Elise and told her to do a *grand jeté*. He lifted her. Then she did two *pirouettes* and he stopped her facing the audience. "Now that looked easy, didn't it?" The boys muttered affirmatively. "Well, just to show you how hard it is, I want a volunteer to come down here and try it." No one volunteered. "Look, don't be scared. All you have to do is lift her, carry her a few feet, put her down gently—that's important—then wait for her to do two turns, and stop her facing forward." He demonstrated again. "Now, a volunteer. No, wait, I don't want a volunteer, I want Jason!"

The crowd roared. I had grown up with Jason. He was my first friend. We fought over the same girl in nursery school. Then, at about age fourteen, something horrible happened. Jason grew, not only tall but big too. His chest broadened out to make room for the steel muscles that were forming. He started shaving, and the girls loved him. So naturally our close friendship died. Now Jason was the most popular student in the tenth grade. Known for his playboy qualities, his strength, and his humor, Jason was the number-one class ham. His head popped out from the bleachers while screams and applause resounded. Jason marched out onto the gym floor.

"All right, Jason," my father addressed him, "you'd better take off your jacket."

"All right, Jacques." Jason mimicked his voice. He threw off his jacket, revealing a bright yellow alligator shirt. The shirt was so tight it might have exploded if he flexed just one muscle.

My father brought Elise over. "O.K., Jason, she's all yours."

"*Aaarrrrrgg!*" Jason growled, rubbing his hands together and walking toward Elise. The boys cheered. He had no trouble with the *grand jeté*. Like a sack of potatoes he hauled her up, walked three steps, and plunked her down. Everyone applauded. Jason acknowledged the audience with one of those "no problem" expressions.

"Good," my father yelled. "Now do the *pirouette.* She's going to turn twice and you stop her facing front."

Poor Jason, how was he to know? He stepped in very close to Elise with his arms outstretched to support her. Just as he stepped in behind her, it happened. As Elise rounded her second turn, her right knee, which was bent in the *passé* position, slammed into Jason who was standing too close to her. Her knee landed right between his legs. Squealing like a baby mouse, Jason awkwardly sprang backward guarding the wounded area with his hands and showing his embarrassment in his cheeks. It took five minutes for the laughter to subside, and it was years before the story was no longer repeated at lunch. I was rarely teased again about dancing. In fact, as a result, several students previously unknown to me approached me asking, "Are you the one who does ballet?" with a touch of admiration in their voices.

So now it was generally accepted that dancers weren't always gay. Surprisingly, just a small percentage of my classmates had ever actually known anyone gay. That is why the arrival of Kevin was of special notice to me. He joined our class in the tenth grade. He was widely built, muscular, and very gay. I took notice, passed premature judgment, and promptly forgot about him. After a few months a dark fearful rumor swept through the school, "Is Kevin gay?" Assuming that I held knowledge on the subject, several boys put the question to me. "Naturally he is," I assured them. This was not reassuring; in fact, many boys became afraid of Kevin, fearing to even look at him. No one dared be seen sitting next to him at lunch or in class. He became an instant outcast. In each class he attended, he was left sitting on the perimeter of the tight-knit students, like the last remaining piece of a jigsaw puzzle.

Kevin ended up with two acquaintances, not even friends, but people with whom he could talk—Jason and myself. Jason always preceded the rest of us in maturity. He seemed already secure enough so as to be able to befriend Kevin without fear of social chastisement. Since I grew up with ballet, homosexuality was no novelty. I felt no prejudice toward it. Kevin and I would talk about his homosexuality, which was a rare outlet for him—unfortunately, one that he grew addicted to. He began tailing me with increasing frequency. Originally, I was glad to support him, but eventually I learned to dread his company. I plainly disliked him. So what had initially brought philanthropic pleasure soon became a nuisance. Just before I was forced to repudiate him for my own peace of mind, all was resolved. Besides being gay, Kevin was a terrible student. So one school year was the duration of his stay at Collegiate. I felt a little sorry for him and wondered if he would find another person to help him. Apparently he did not. I received six months' worth of phone calls from him, wanting to see me. I hate to lie, but I told him that I was too busy to see him. Finally, he stopped calling. I always felt guilty about having pushed him off. That bothered me. It never seemed fair that I ended up feeling guilt because I had once tried to befriend someone.

The walk to the theater Tuesday morning was a particularly exciting one. It was early and the Lincoln Center Plaza was empty. I stopped in front of the fountain. The little black marble fountain is flanked on three sides by massive white buildings. On the right is Avery Fisher Hall, where almost nightly great musical performances may be heard. The Metropolitan Opera House is centered behind the fountain with two huge Chagall paintings displayed behind the windows in its facade. On the left is the theater that houses the greatest ballet company in the world—the New York State Theater, home of the New York City Ballet. On the wall of the theater was a six-foot-high poster that read across the top: NEW YORK CITY BALLET—SPRING SEASON. Below was a list of the ballets to be performed throughout the May to July season. To the right was another poster. Its bright blue and red colors proclaimed that *Camelot* with Richard Burton would be here in July. A third poster was of the New York City Opera explaining that it was presently performing in the theater.

I had entered the theater countless times, but this morning I entered legally. I was now officially adopted and could truly call this immense theater my home. I was the ninety-eighth dancer presently in the company. I opened the stage door and approached the guard. This time I didn't have to explain that I was my father's son. Now all I had to say to him was, "Good morning."

On route to the New York State Theater (far left). Behind is Avery Fisher Hall (far right). The Metropolitan Opera House is in the center.

School was over forever. As soon as my senior project was approved, school life grew curiously and vitally attractive. I became hesitant to leave and signed up for an English course. This was unrequired, but suddenly I did not wish to hurry my scholastic departure. This literature class met only on Mondays and Wednesdays at 10 A.M. As a New York City Ballet member Monday was my day off, and as for Wednesdays, since the morning company class was not mandatory it could be sacrificed. In fact, I would be glad to miss it. The title of "company member" did not diminish my apprehension of the company class. It seemed that only when you were a member did the other dancers really start to size you up. I felt they all looked at me to determine where I would end up. Would I excel? Or was I a loser? Thoughts about the future did not cross my mind; what really mattered was whether these people would like me. I did not simply glide right in to the company with the ease I had anticipated. The first rehearsal with the company was eviscerating.

There are eight boys and eight girls in the fourth movement of Balanchine's *Tchaikovsky's Suite No. 3*. I was called to the main hall to learn this ballet. The main hall is the largest studio in the theater; a gray square room with no windows. When I arrived seven boys and eight girls were wandering around awaiting the commencement of the rehearsal. I did not know where to go. Should I sit down or try and open a conversation with one of the dancers? I found myself standing by the piano in the corner of the studio pretending to be interested in the sheet music that was lying atop it.

With brisk little steps Rosemary walked in. She was the ballet mistress and taught most of the Balanchine ballets. She is a small woman with short dark hair and sharp quick movements. She used to be a dancer in the company. The rehearsal began. I learned the steps with average swiftness, but was tentative to dance them with full energy. All of the other dancers were marking the steps.

"Marking" is the dancers' term used when one merely indicates the movements of a dance without much effort. An official label for laziness.

Rosemary sat on top of the ballet barre with her back resting against the mirror. She was probably wondering, "He seems to be a fairly quick study, but can he lift the girls? Will he fall apart on stage?" I shrank with the feeling that her eyes were always appraising me. I felt so young. I was the youngest male member, but the age difference was not so great. Still, I felt like an apprentice to the pros. Why did I feel so damned out of place? I looked in the mirror. I had the same slender look about me as the rest of the men. I was wearing sweat pants and a T shirt, as were the others. In appearance I blended, but with every breath I felt like a weak-kneed colt placed among a herd of Thoroughbreds. So far *Suite No. 3* was the only ballet I was called to rehearse. I would have one week before opening night to accustom myself to the steps.

Since I had no other rehearsals I went apartment hunting. It was not any strong need to leave home that sent me out for my own place, but now I was getting a regular salary and the money burned in my pocket. An apartment was now an affordable luxury.

All this was simply handed to me. These things I wanted were mine almost before I really wanted them. As swift as that a new life was beginning. I thought to myself, "This is where real life begins, right?"

MAY

Candy Cane—The Nutcracker.

The commencement of something is exhilarating; so is the end. Opening a new book freshly purchased brings exciting pleasure, and closing it and putting it on the shelf also evokes satisfaction. That space between start and finish determines if the book is any good, whether it is worth putting on the shelf or tossing away.

In the same sense, mornings are optimistic. They are the beginnings—filled with the exhilaration of uncertainty and expectation. There is vitality in the morning knowing that anything might occur.

However, the night fails to produce pleasure like the final page of a book. Night is indeed an ending, but it is not the finish—as if one has completed a book but knows there is a sequel.

I prefer the mornings and claim to be a morning person. Although often I may sleep through it, the point is not the hour of reveille, because, whatever the hour, it's a definite starting line.

The distance from my parents' house to the theater is about ten blocks. There are several old and interesting buildings along the way, but most are obstructed by newer, taller, rickety constructions. That describes New York—a city of elegant antiquities blanketed by progress.

If one makes the effort to look, there is something worth seeing on most every block. Native New Yorkers never look. They concentrate solely on their path. A tourist is easily distinguished by his apparent appreciaton of the surroundings. New Yorkers can penetrate crowds and transverse streets without seeming aware of traffic. Nevertheless, they sense everything as though they had radar, and can dangerously zigzag across an intractable intersection with only subconscious navigation. I have seen New Yorkers walk an intricate sinuous path down a sidewalk in expert avoidance of the dog droppings. Like an army man holding a mine detector far out in front so as to avoid disaster, the New Yorker has a built-in detector and needs not even look.

However, last year the dog population was so great that even New Yorkers were to be seen falling prey to pet remains. So the "scoop" law was passed requiring all owners to clean up after their pups. This was a practical idea, I thought, but what about when it rained? Or was cold? Who would comply then?

Now, a year later, my skepticism has been proved ill-founded—the streets are practically dirt-free. The New Yorker's built-in detector has become obsolete.

I always feel proud when on some snowy windy winter morning, I see an old lady, stiff with arthritis, bending over with a piece of newspaper to clean up after her pooch. New Yorkers really do love their city.

Tonight the New York City Opera ended its engagement at the New York State Theater. I know this because a friend of mine returned my little gray-and-white Greek worry beads. My friend sings in the chorus of the opera. When the opera season concludes, she has no work and is forced to become an usher while NYCB occupies the theater. I have visited her there often, seeking her out when I used to sneak in to watch the ballet. Her name is Pannia, and she is quite beautiful and surprisingly slim for an opera singer.

Often female opera singers are of enormous proportions. I once entered the elevator with four of them. I had a cold and was coughing relentlessly. Their bodies were of such immensity that I had no direction in which to cough without fear of jaculating my virus upon one of them. "That's a bad cough!" the bovine blonde said to me. "You're lucky you're not a singer. If you were, you'd be in trouble!"

I looked at her and smiled politely. I hoped that my smile was a convincing cover for my contradictory thoughts which were, "You're lucky you're not a dancer.

If you were, you'd be in trouble!" Pannia is the beautifully anomalous exception.

I had found the gray-and-white beads and had given them to her. She hung them on her makeup place for good luck. Presently, as she was moving out of the theater she returned them to me saying, "Now you need the good luck." It was agreed that as the State Theater alternates companies Pannia and I would exchange the beads. Tomorrow I will have my own makeup place to hang them on.

This morning I dashed off to the theater at nine o'clock. Even though it was so early, half of the makeup places were already claimed. There are about ten separate makeup places on either side of the huge table in the boys' dressing room. Each boy gets his own place with a built-in mirror surrounded by lights. This morning there was little choice among the places. Several black theater cases were already propped on the table. These marked a claim to that spot by the owner of the bag. Soon I would also receive a theater case, but at present my name, written on a piece of paper, sufficed to claim the spot I desired. There were seven places left, yet my choice was further limited because many of the older dancers have unspoken rights to these places due to seniority. Seniority outranks the first-come first-served law. It matters little where I sit, but whom I sit next to is very important! I circled the room reading the names on the theater cases to locate a suitable habitat. There was a vacant place between Luke and Alex. I liked them both, and Luke was a favorite of mine. He is older than I and has been in the company for eight years. He looks much like the actor Oliver Reed, with big broad shoulders, thick black hair, and heavy gray eyes. He's quite interesting-looking and a little crazy I believe. On the other side was Alex. He is but a few years older than I, and entered the company last year.

He is very quiet. He is gay. That's fine with me, for the gay tend to be more neat.

In big block letters I printed my name on a paper towel and fitted it between Alex and Luke. Then I hung the worry beads from one of the lights. Now I had my own place. Already I felt partial toward it and worried about acquiring the same one next season. I ran up to the wardrobe room and pilfered a few coat hangers—even though it was my first year I was already acquainted with some of the tricks of the trade.

Every night the ballet mistress, Rosemary Dunleavy, makes a tape recording of the following day's rehearsals. And every night I call this tape. I must dial the number several times before getting through. It seems that all the dancers call at the same time. Sometimes when I'm out very late at a party, I wait until returning home early in the morning to call the tape. Sure enough, it's busy! On those nights I hang up the phone wondering who else is up at that hour; what party did they go to? Nevertheless, when finally receiving a ring, rather than the busy signal buzz, it is always exciting to hear what ballets are to be learned the next day.

Today the tape called me to learn Balanchine's *Kammermusik*. This ballet involves eight corps boys, and two principal couples. I was unimpressed upon hearing from the tape that I would be learning *Kammermusik*. Oh, I didn't mind, but I have a druthers for a Tchaikovsky melody, and a love story. *Kammermusik* is the music of Hindemith, and the choreography is totally abstract.

At noon sixteen boys arrived in the main hall rehearsal room. Eight boys were there to teach, the other eight to learn. I became Luke's understudy. He had been in the ballet since its creation, and was glad to be getting an understudy. He handed me a piece of gum, "Chewing helps you concentrate, and you'll need lots of help for this ballet." He was right! Never has there been such an intractable ballet to learn. There are two reasons for the extreme difficulty. First, the choreography is so unorthodox that few steps are recognizable classroom steps. Movements one could never dream of are required. Secondly, there is no simple melody to follow, just frantic, nightmare music. "You must count constantly," Luke advised me. "Three fives and a seven, then comes your first step. After that you wait two sixes and a three, or one six and a nine, whatever is easiest for you."

I was getting a headache. It was so damned mental. The effort that went into the counting alone was exhausting. To me dancing was much more mindless enjoyment. Of course the mind functioned, but I never would consciously *think*. I never had to count the music; I just listened. I never thought of the steps; I just did them. All this distressed me. It was too much in the head, and this sort of intellectual focus would spoil the thrill. After about a half hour of struggling to command the counts and steps we were to try it with the music. The original eight boys demonstrated. Then it was our turn. I stood ready, waiting for Rosemary to start us off.

Rosie stood at the front of the studio with her hand raised like a flag starter at a race. She is an impressive woman. She possesses a computerlike mind with seemingly limitless abilities. She can instantly recall any step from any ballet upon request.

Like the gates banging open at the race track, we sprang into action when Rosie said, "GO!" It was a race— the body racing to keep up with the mind racing to keep pace with the music. What a horror! In less than thirty seconds we were done, breathing heavily. With the great surprise of realization, I felt thrilled! Not only had I made it through without any mistakes, but I loved it! Such exhilaration!

In the game of basketball, upon rare occasion there occurs a moment during a game when you jump high, twisting your body to clear a path to the basket for the ball. Then you let the ball fly from your hands. The shot taken is quite some length from the basket and the preparation is so unorthodox that everyone wonders why you took it. But the instant that ball leaves your fingertips you know it's right! You feel so confident that you needn't even watch to see if it scores; you know it will! They are rare, these few times when everything comes together so precisely that it cannot help but be perfect. This half-a-second feeling of perfection as the ball takes its flight describes my feeling through the entire thirty seconds of dancing *Kammermusik*. The steps were fit to complement the music so perfectly that to complete them successfully was to become part of the music.

I have continually been told of the greatness of Balanchine, and have always believed it without truly discovering why. Now it seems so obvious. Balanchine has said that the music dictates the choreography. Today I felt like another instrument in the orchestra, an appendage to the music. Fantastic! This is something so special, like a great book that one savors slowly forestalling its completion. But with the ballet, there is not finality, it may always be created anew, differently, like stepping into a book and taking the place of a character.

A five-minute break was announced. Many boys dashed to the elevators to purchase sodas and candy from the lower level.

Rosie went to the pianist, "When the boys come back we'll go into the second movement."

"Luke," I yelled, "how many movements do we have to learn?"

"Six," he answered, "and the first was the easiest."

I swallowed heavily at this information. Luke walked toward the elevator with fifty cents in his hand for a soda.

"Luke," I yelled again, grabbing a quarter from my bag, "while you're down there, would you buy me a pack of gum? I'll need it!"

A free moment in the dressing room.

There are so many beautiful women in this company it's overwhelming! I am often late for morning class, and slip into the studio after the dancers have already begun *pliés*. However, on occasion when I arrive early, I spend my few free minutes regarding other dancers. With maybe one or two exceptions, all the women are beautiful! Truly stunning! Each possesses individual glamour. Yet it is a beauty recognizable as belonging to a dancer. They all have strong slim bodies. The elegance they possess is simple beauty, plain beauty, with no embellishments. I smile at my father across the studio. He knows my thoughts. We laugh out loud to ourselves.

When Mr. B. watches class we all tremble fearing he might find some fault with our dancing, or perhaps he is studying the way we work. I'll bet that his prevalent thoughts are: "Look at all the beautiful women!"

One would, in justice to their beauty, expect that each one of these choice morsels was engaged to a tall handsome man. Not so! The dancers' unpredictable and relentless schedule leaves very little time to get acquainted with outside men. And if perchance one does find a compatible man outside the company, the difficulties in sustaining a relationship are tremendous. These girls work long hours in varying timetables each day. A man would need to be independently wealthy and have no other occupation but to fit himself into the girl's schedule. Most of the ballerinas bemoan the necessity of either picking a man from the company or going without. Unfortunately for them, much of the male contingent is gay.

Fortunately for me, I am not!

They used to say that the ballet was the best place for a homosexual to find a mate. It seems to me that the arrangement is more advantageous for the straight man. The ratio of beautiful women to eligible men is quite favorable. Not all these beauties, I regret, flock to me, but at least I may admire them firsthand and smirk with my father at my lecherous thoughts.

Although I had rehearsed and repeated all the steps countless times, fear still made me jittery. I felt weak. This was to be my first performance—one of the eight boys in the corps of the "Theme" section of Tchaikovsky's *Suite No. 3*. I paced around backstage awaiting my entrance. Luke was standing in the wings watching the dancers already on stage. I went to him for a little consoling.

He laughed, and said, "Listen, after you've done this as long as I have, the excitement wears off. But I remember my first time." There was silence while he was recollecting, then he emitted a slow cackle of a laugh. "When I first did this I was thrown in for Bobby, who had torn ligaments in his calf that afternoon. So I had to learn it in just a few hours. I was not afraid, I was a pretty confident guy, pretty damn sure of myself. So I went out there in a blaze of glory. Even though it was only a corps part, I felt like everyone was looking at me to see how I would fare. I was carrying on as if the role had been mine for years, with energy and gusto. Then, when it came time to stand on the side while the principals dar_ed, I did it proudly. I was in front and knew that in back of me were five boys who had to line themselves up behind me, so I stood proud; a strong example. The next step was an enormous jumping combination into the center of the stage. I flexed my muscles as I stood waiting for the proper music to set myself flying. I waited, reviewing in my mind what Rosemary had told me, *"Wait for the second repeat of the melody, then count eight threes, then start the jump step."* So I waited for the repeat of the melody. When I first heard the melody I smiled to myself and waited calmly for the repeat. Then the music changed and the smile left my face. Something was terribly wrong. Where was the second repeat? The melody seemed to have vanished. What happened? I wanted to turn around and see what the other boys were doing, but I couldn't. I forced myself to straighten up and pretend that everything was all right, that the melody would return. But damn, that music played on with a melody I did not recognize. 'Luke, you're late!' I heard someone yell from the wings. 'You missed it!' I panicked. I turned and looked behind me. The boys weren't there! Not only had I missed the jump step but everything after it also! The boys had already exited, and there I was standing so proud while everyone else was gone!" Again Luke laughed his slow drawling laugh. "I'll never forget it. To this day I still sweat abnormally while awaiting that melody."

Luke's story wasn't the comfort I had sought, but I was relieved not to be in the front, as he was. One of the qualities most amiable about Luke is that although he takes his work seriously, he never loses a sense of humor about it. I don't like it when people take life too seriously. Nothing is so grave that humor cannot be found in it. We are so spoiled, we live so easily, free of so many of the hardships that plagued people of the past. A person who really had a tough life would gasp incredulously at some of the stern faces around here. I probably annoy the other dancers with my optimistic effervescence.

I was located at the back of the line of boys so I could follow easily. But I didn't feel the need to follow, I knew the steps perfectly! After all I had been rehearsing practically nothing but these steps for two weeks. The three preceding movements seemed interminable, but at last the music changed and our entrance was forthcoming. I took my partner and, determined to act professionally, calmly wished her good luck. Oh, but I was so nervous. I glanced at Luke in the wing in front of me. He looked so coolly professional. He returned my glance just before our entrance. He smiled, his eyes glittered, and he cried, *"Merde!"*—We ran out onto the stage grinning. I held my partner's hand, feeling insecure in every movement. I smiled and danced and smiled, and smiled. I peeked across at the boys on the other side of the stage. None of them were smiling! Were we not supposed to smile in this ballet? Nobody told me! No, it must be that they just don't want to smile. "Well, hell, I want to smile," I assured myself, and reared the Cheshire grin. Then panic struck. I did a terrible thing that I would later learn is a fatal mistake. I thought ahead about what the upcoming steps were. I stood grinning, trying to remember just what that last jump combination was. Did it start with the right foot or the left? I wasn't sure. The more I struggled to remember the less time there was before I would have to execute it. The less time, the more panicky I became and the less coherently I could think. I was finally reduced to a pitiful cry for help, sweating profusely.

Then came the moment. Oh, if only I could have run off stage! All the boys started the step. I followed, slightly behind the rest. And then much to my relief, I knew! I knew exactly what to do—even though my mind was flustered, my body performed it naturally. How wonderful! "Ha ha!" I laughed as I did the final *double tour*, the grin still beaming on my face, even after the curtain went down.

"Take three big steps, jump, throwing your right leg as high as you can. Then bring the left leg up to meet the right. From there you must land on the right with the left in *arabesque*." This he demonstrated to me. Mischa—Mikhail Baryshnikov—had joined the company a few months ago; this was the first time I had spoken to him. I tried this step. "That's not so hard," I bragged. "Ah," Mischa smiled, "do it again, but this time spin twice in the air before you land!" I looked around the room. It was empty except for Ellen, who was sewing shoes. I wanted to make sure that as few people as possible heard me. I laughed at him, the leap he had described sounded so impossible that I could only stand and laugh. He quickly silenced me by taking three big steps, throwing his right leg into the air, bringing the left to meet it, SPINNING TWICE in the air and landing in *arabesque!* I said nothing; what could I say? My embarrassed silence was relieved, for Mischa left the studio and went down to the stage to rehearse. He smiled to himself as he left. He left me alone with this incredible leap. I tried it and fell. I tried it again and fell and fell, and fell. Frustrated and angry, I stomped out of the studio while Ellen laughed. I went directly to O'Neal's for lunch, following the dancers' motto: "When in doubt—EAT!"

Rehearsal Schedule   5/17
Class—10:45–11:45   Taras
New Ballet 12:00–2:00   C. d'Amboise—Robbins

Panic!
Two hours alone in the main rehearsal room with only Jerry Robbins and a pianist! Without warning my name appears on the schedule, and I don't sleep all night!

In the main rehearsal hall. Barbara Seibert is underneath.

What could he wish to do for two hours? Whatever his design, I wanted to be ready for anything, so by eleven-thirty I was warmed up and anxious.

At twelve on the dot, he walked in. Seeing him somehow calmed me. He reminds me of a favorite grandfather, wonderfully young in appearance and wise in conversation. He walked toward me. I must have been carrying that Cheshire grin for I always do when I'm nervous. "How are you?" he asked. "Fine," was my eloquent answer. "Listen," he continued, "this is a little something I want to choreograph. I doubt you'll ever perform it, I just want to play around with it for fun." "Fine," I repeated. "So," he began, facing the mirror, "you start like this . . ."

The two hours passed in agony. At the end of the

rehearsal he videotaped the dance and thanked me. Afterward I slithered away to bury my head. (Why do we always want to be alone when we are feeling worthless?) I had danced so badly! All the years of classes seemed to have abandoned me. Jerry was very nice about it. He waited patiently while I fumbled over the steps he demonstrated. His kindness made it worse. He has such a reputation for sternness, if he had gotten mad at me I might have felt a little less abased. Self-pity is the most unattractive state. I spent those two hours in misery. I never expected that. When I'm involved with a group I usually crave singular attention, yet when I get it . . . I balk, and look for excuses. I should not have been there. I wasted his time.

A rehearsal with Jerome Robbins.

Often, when class is scheduled for 10 A.M. it is hard for me to quit the bed early enough to become coherent in time. Although both mind and body may be conscious before ten, they are slow to grasp responsibility for themselves. This morning, however, some unknown peculiarity rendered me wide-eyed long before class time. I ate a very large breakfast, read the paper, and still was early for class. Upon my premature arrival the studio was dark and empty. It was a bit spooky. I lay down on the floor and began doing leg raises . . .

When I woke up the room was full of dancers. There is a terrifying moment of confusion when you wake up and don't know how long you've slept. I feared that perhaps I had slept right through the entire barre exercises— how embarrassing! No one seemed to notice me. I glanced at the wall clock—hooray, I had only dozed twenty minutes. It was five minutes before ten, and class always started five minutes late. I climbed up off the floor and stood by the barre. "Class is fairly crowded," I remarked to myself, as I appraised the other dancers. One woman in the back of the studio attracted my notice by her desperate avoidance of attention. It was Emily, sweet Emily.

Emily had arrived at the School of American Ballet at the age of eighteen. Her mother was a dance teacher in Florida. Ever since Emily could recall her mother told her that she was to be the greatest ballerina ever. At eighteen her mother finally allowed her to come to New York. "Mama" quit her teaching job and moved to NYC with her daughter. Indeed, Emily was a talented dancer and was taken into the company directly. She had one of those happy faces like the faces we learned to draw as children—a large round circle with a big smile. Attached to that circle was long black hair. She would have looked even cuter with short hair, but "Mummy" would never let her cut it. Emily had the longest eyelashes I had ever seen, they were of such length and thickness that she could snuff a candle with a wink.

At twelve years old, I had had a deep crush on her. She was not very tall but neither was I. Despite the impossible age difference I still hoped she would be my wife one day.

Now I looked across the studio at her and was deeply disturbed. She has never excelled as a dancer. Oh she is very good, but not the star material her mother promised. "Mummy" still lives with her and hounds her.

Highly specialized fields often have specialized problems common only to them, and there is a specialized disease that afflicts dancers. Although it is not really a physical disease, it works the same way. It sets in quietly and gradually infects a person, changing him or her. It is sparked by dissatisfaction, then kindled by guilt and shame. As it increases it becomes almost a self-hate and even attempts to overthrow one's sense of pride and worth. It often occurs in those dancers whose exclusive desire is to be the "ballet star." They are talented and well on their way, but fail for some reason they do not see; cannot understand. The disease now snatches them.

For these dancers the only criterion for value and self-worth is dance. There is no other standard of merit. If they don't "make it" in the dance, then they are failures as people—or so they feel.

In college, a popular student is not necessarily the one with impeccable grades, nor the dexterous sportsman. Often a student unexcelling in any common mode is admired and envied for those other qualities that he or she possesses.

But the dancer's disease clouds the mind so as to allow only one way to success, only one gauge of importance.

Emily has this disease and feels that if she does not excel and prove herself in the dance, she is a failure in life—a disgrace.

At this point the disease takes over. This miserable failing guilt eats at the victim. She grows ashamed of herself and yet at the same time there is pride struggling to survive. She will be quick to defend her profession, yet ashamed of her performance in it. A battle rages between pride and shame.

Every day the diseased are faced with their failing. Every morning in class they must shamefully look at themselves in the mirror while at the same time the mirror reflects the other dancers, and the younger ones who have already passed them by. Now, like the prostitute who is shamed by her reflection, these diseased do what they can to hide from themselves. Thick dark makeup is applied, layers of leg warmers are wrapped around preceding layers, and a crazy intensity sets in, like the last desperate struggle of a drowning woman who makes a frantic lurch—but has no idea how to swim.

Emily used to stand up at the front of the class wearing only tights and leotards, but now she slithers in the back with scarfs and layers of colored leg warmers. She has gloomy heavily made-up eyes that won't look straight at you anymore. Her happy face is masked with sorrow. I cannot bear to look at her. It hurts me. There she is in the back of the studio doing some kooky exercises which she has learned from some mystic ballet teacher. Emily will hardly stray from the back of the studio for the entire class. Everyone will ignore her as she tries to ignore herself.

My father just walked into class. He distracted me from thoughts of Emily; I am glad for it. It's rare for him to be this late. I am amazed that he comes at all! He must have an operation; he has dislocated his middle toe and it will not heal. They are frightening-looking—his toes.

They represent a strong argument against ballet as a career. He never had a good arch. In order to make his feet look cleaner and neater, he pressed them into tight ballet shoes, always wearing several sizes too small. Now that he is well over forty, the results appear. Like gnarled claws his toes are bent, twisted hooks that cannot straighten. At the Hospital for Special Surgery they plan to completely remove the joint from the middle toe of both his feet. They will then straighten out these jointless toes and sew them to the neighboring ones. Webbed feet! My father has reached the stage where all the years of physical abuse begin to take their toll.

He told me about it one night. He spoke not with sorrow but with a kind of soberness that one might use in speaking of a past love:

"When I was younger, each day was a growth, an improvement. At the end of each year I could proudly look back and realize that I was dancing better than the year before. Each year I could do things that I had never attempted before. There were new ballets and new challenges, while the old ballets were getting easier and more fun. It was a wonderful time, the best time. But then the growth process stops, and a stalemate occurs. Although things are no worse, neither are they any better! And believe me, it's just a short time thereafter when things begin to deteriorate. First goes the stamina, then the elevation. It sneaks up on you, and it's like a slap of cold water in the face. One night, as you're taking off your makeup, you realize that you danced better a couple of years ago! From there each year gets worse, until you just stop thinking about if you're good anymore, and all you worry about is if you can do it. There are still roles that I dance better than anyone. But I know that it's not what it used to be—not all it could be. It kills some of the fun of dancing. God, if I could go on dancing forever, I would. But I'll go on as long as I feel I bring something special to the stage."

For now, he just does the best he can, with much pain I'm sure. He winks at me from across the studio, we both look at the clock, and then at the door through which John Taras should be entering to start the class. Mr. B. stuck his head through that same door last month. I have not seen him since. He looked into class, hired me, and disappeared. Apparently he is having heart trouble and needs surgery. I am so frightened that he might die. *Aahhh!* I should not even say it! No one in the company dares even to think of it. If the subject is brought up, people quickly turn away saying, "Let's not talk about it." I feel the same.

I have known Balanchine since I was little. But I never desired his mentorship as I do now. Just as I never wanted to learn until I was leaving school. Now that I am ready, Mr. B. is not here. Oh, how often it happens that when things are available we don't desire them, but when they are gone—eureka! Desire flourishes.

John Taras walked through the door and for a second I thought it was Mr. B. How could I have been mistaken? I suppose it was like a mirage, the dehydrated man's illusionary oasis.

Even though I am very happy with Luke and Alex as my dressing-room mates, I am certainly not unaffected by the dancers on the other side of the dressing room. I overheard Bobby and Sebastian talking about the women they had conquered. Neither man ever ranked very high with me, and their conversation unredeemingly lowered them in my estimation. Bobby was speaking of a girl he had entertained the previous night. Sebastian asked, "So did you get her?" At that my stomach twisted. Bobby answered, "Yeah, I porked her good!" "Jesus Christ!" I wanted to scream!

"Porked her!" What an ignoble thing to say. How vile he seemed to me. Like a slimy insect that steals goodies in the dark and rushes back to tell his fellow roach. Oh, men can be the basest of caitiffs! They are so reduced by their weaknesses, and put such importance on status and machismo!

These two guys could meet and seduce a woman without a second thought. They only worry about whom they can tell in the morning. To them there is little difference between one woman and the next—but for blond or black hair. Everything is physical to them; everything a sensual fulfillment.

I think women are truly the superior beings. As a whole they are far more sensitive, reliable, and appreciative than men. They are more resourceful. They outlive men too!

I'll bet if it had been all girls instead of boys that were stranded on the island in *Lord of the Flies*, when the rescue ship arrived they would all have been found safe and sufficiently prepared for survival, unlike the boys who turned wild, killing each other off. Another important difference is that women seek to understand men. Most men know very little about the women they are with, and because of this, women can manipulate men. It's as if men were nearsighted and unable to see beyond a fixed distance.

For example—sitting at a table are a man and a woman. The woman is criticizing the man. She calls him greedy. As she speaks thoughts are racing through the man's head:

1. He raises high defenses, saying to himself: "Look at her talking. She couldn't get another date if she tried. She's lucky that I'm even sitting here . . ."

2. If the man has a little sensitivity he might take the criticism to heart and wonder: "Am I really greedy?"

When the roles are reversed, at the same table with the same man and woman, and this time the man is calling the woman greedy. She thinks:

1. "Am I really greedy? What gave him that impression?"

2. "He should talk, he's more greedy than I."

And here is where the woman shows her difference, she takes the thought process one step further:

3. She wonders: *"Why is he saying this to me?"* She seeks to understand the man. And the better she understands the man's point of view, the more value his criticism carries. The man, however, seems only concerned with himself. And so women gain knowledge of how men think, and the better one understands how something works, the more dexterous is one's handling of it.

Consequently, I am never manipulated by men, but I am a sucker for women. I may even be keenly aware of a woman's maneuverings. Still, there is little to be done about it because if one pushes the right button the machine will run. I will continue to claim women supreme because my proclamation raises me slightly above the great mass of men. Although a woman might stoop to be an animal, she would never be an insect! She would never "pork" a man!

I cannot relate to people who look admiringly at themselves in the mirror. They remind themselves of how terrific they look. I swear, all I see are faults! All the unfortunate features are revealed through the mirror.

We took the final bow for Jerome Robbins' *Interplay* ten minutes ago. The effect of this performance has depressed me before my makeup mirror. One soothing consolation is that Jerry wasn't here to see this performance. I tried my damnedest out on the stage, and actually performed quite well, but unless a good performance is supported by some good dancing it becomes distasteful, ugly, lots of dessert but no meal. A year ago I danced *Interplay* in the School of American Ballet graduation program. What fun it was—the careless enjoyment of dancing. But as we mature and gain increased knowledge of the dance, we recognize new faults and new aspirations.

A year ago little mattered but enjoying myself. But now it was horrible. I hated dancing *Interplay* because I know I'm not good enough. I'm riding on a smile, not ability, and that is terrible!

It's ironic that the knowledge I have gained about dancing has killed some of the pleasure of it. The more I learn, the more I can see my limitations and the less happy I feel on stage. I cannot do things that I don't feel I do well. There is no enjoyment in that. Some people aren't bothered by being bad, but I'll have none of it.

In Interplay.

JUNE

In Tchaikovsky Suite #2.

June 6 was Collegiate's graduation day. I received permission to attend, missing a day's rehearsals. During this last semester I had gained an increased popularity among schoolmates, so now I regretted school's ending.

I was nervous walking up all those stairs to shake hands and receive my diploma. Oh yes, the graceful dancer could hardly walk. Walking suddenly became a most awkward movement. It might have been better if I could have danced my way up the stairs.

One never believes that he will regret the finish of school. Older people always tell us that some day we will fondly remember those school days as the most exciting. I already felt that way, and almost wished to be going off to college as all my classmates were.

The worst blow of all was that my girlfriend of six months was going off to Boston where she would, in advancing to college, flip from being a senior to being a freshman again. Do they call them freshwomen? If not, it's just a matter of time.

Jason, good old Jason, was off to California to a university where he could get suntanned as well as educated.

I would not have traded places with any of them. But people hate to give up things. We are reluctant to throw anything out. By my decision to dance I was forsaking college. Oh, certainly, you can always return to college later in life, but it's not the same as when you are young. In turn, my classmates were envious of me, not that they wanted to dance, but simply because I knew what I wanted to do. They were terrified about not knowing. It is terrifying. It is one of the hardest things a person faces, and one of the most vital—finding something that interests you enough to spend your life pursuing it. Without that idea or that goal it would be very difficult to ever be happy. All one needs to be happy is a simple approachable goal, along with the ability to pursue it, and under it all the energy to set yourself in motion.

This is the simplest way to look at it. That really is all that is needed, barring unforeseen circumstances. But I wonder if my goal is truly as divine as it seems. My parents fear that my overexposure to the ballet has blinded me so that I see all of the glory but none of the sweat involved. Perhaps they are right. But it's too late now. Two fellow students sang Billy Joel's "I've Loved These Days." The song probably touched me more than most because these days for me were truly over.

What parents hope for when they send their children to school is that beyond the learning of basic scholastic skills the school will teach them the value of right and wrong. The school takes on the responsibility of disciplining the students in the ways of right and wrong. A child grows up to believe that there is an unwritten list of goods and bads, of do's and don'ts. All they have to do is learn the list to know how one should behave.

Imagine a child's confusion when he reads a philosopher and wholeheartedly agrees with the convictions presented. Then he picks up a different book and reads a completely contradictory explanation. Much to his horror he finds that he agrees with both!

How can that be? How can they both be right?

This same process continues and increases until the youngster has no idea about what he once knew as right and wrong. He is not prepared for this and resents that he has been misled by his *wise* elders.

"Do not be selfish."
"Don't live for others."

"Live for the moment."
"Prepare for the future."

"Be responsible."
"Be carefree."

44

I was taught: "Be nice to everyone. Be especially kind to the girl you like best."

How many times has it happened that the girl you like best and treat with profound adoration falls for the bastard who treats her with cruelty! This shakes up a young man. He is at a loss to reconcile these opposites.

Soon he learns the undesirable fact that affection, preceded with cruelty, more often than not wins greater favor and respect from women.

When I was young—well, younger than I am now—I firmly believed my mother to be an angel. Although she was not religious, if there was a God he would, despite her blasphemy, ordain her an angel.

She is what I later learned to call an altruist.

"Be nice to everybody and everybody will like you." That is what she believes, and it works for her. I do not know of anyone who dislikes my mother. Even people she may dislike receive nothing but kindness and reciprocate it. That is truly admirable. There is no one else about whom I could say this.

I wanted to be like her and emulated the angel, but was continually distressed by intensely selfish feelings. They came upon me instinctively. I was never perfect as I wanted to be.

My father is what is called an egoist, not to be confused with an egotist. He is not greedy. There is no grabbing for more than his share, yet there is a determination to have his share. He is an independent, confident individual, a very generous man, but generous because he likes to be. Rarely would the egoist do anything against his liking to please another, and never for one he did not like.

As I grew older I found myself emulating qualities of my father. I find his way of life equally as admirable and attractive as my mother's, perhaps even more attractive. But I myself am neither—and both. I am torn between opposites that cannot be reconciled—a keen awareness of other people's feelings and a contempt for this concern. How can one say *black* is better than *white?*

But what have I done? I am searching for the correct way to aim my life—the RIGHT way—yet have just claimed the absurdity and impossibility of a right and wrong!

Well, I suppose we *must* have good and bad spelled out. Everyone must define his *own* morals. So that is what I must do . . . but let us not pretend that the ways are set and fixed. Don't preach this to our children!

It is 1:14 P.M.
At 1:12—I ordered the O'Neals' Baloon burger.
At 1:22—it will arrive in its little red basket.
By 1:25—it's finished.
For the next ten minutes my stomach will attempt to reverse the chef's work—separating bun from burger, from tomato, from ketchup, from salt and pepper, dividing fat from proteins, carbohydrates . . . Then twenty minutes will remain, that is if I don't want dessert. Don't want dessert? How absurd!

So all food should be consumed and the check paid by 1:45, leaving me fifteen minutes to return for my *Kammermusik* rehearsal. There are so many of these damnable rehearsals, and I still have not learned the whole ballet.

O'Neals' is a very popular restaurant as it is located on Columbus Avenue directly across the street from the stage entrance. My table gives me an unobstructed view of the dancers going in and out of the New York State Theater. Every time one of the female dancers leaves the theater she passes by the window—and catches my eye by the sleek quality of her movement. Oh, I envy those who are leaving now, they are probably finished for the day, but awaiting me are two hours in the foggy fluorescent lighting of the main hall studio. I should *want* to go back! The rehearsals should be exhilarating. But instead, I would like nothing—I mean *nothing*—more than to rest quietly all afternoon, eating and drinking. Something's wrong here.

Perhaps my parents' fear of my overexposure to dance is well-founded. One feels on trial here. In my imagination there are voices whispering: "You were given so much, and look at how little you did with it." When I hear these voices I want to disappear, to run back to Collegiate and play basketball. I feel like I'm racing to catch up to where I should be. For example, fortune deals me *Interplay*. People say, "How lucky you are!" Certainly that is true, only I am not yet ready for it. I am premature, like an apprentice given the task of a professional, in the meanwhile turning disrelishful of the trade. Will I ever catch up? If I do, will I then be given another role and tested harder? Is that the way one climbs upward? I always thought one was good *first*, then gained advancement through merit. What does it all matter? The point is not to be a great dancer or famous or wealthy, but to be happy. That is the only important thing; being that there is no God. (Well . . . a little fame and fortune wouldn't hurt.)

There it is. All that can be done is to make oneself as happy as possible.

So can this ballet life give me the happiness I crave?

I love dancing surely, but the preparation that is involved—the rehearsing, the classes—often cools that affinity. The time spent working is far greater than the time spent performing.

Are the spoils worth the hunt?

I have seen too many dancers discover in their late twenties that they are miserable dancing. But they don't leave! No, they remain because now they are older and collecting pleasant paychecks. They are too afraid to leave. They waited for themselves to *grow* happy, to acquire contentment. But all this procrastinating proved only to soften their youthful guts and draw from them the courage necessary to save themselves.

I want to realize *now* if this is to be my fate. I want to be certain before I get older, before I grow dependent on that paycheck. And then, if necessary, I can do whatever is needed to start another life.

One universal trait shared by dancers is a constant complaining about excessive work and minor ailments. I, too, admittedly, indulge in complaint. Yet, it's so foolish a waste of time. Nothing is ever gained, but then nothing is really sought. It becomes simply a habitual unconscious part of the day, like asking, "How are you?" to a familiar face on the street, although you don't really care. I must practice getting out of this vice. No one wants to hear the problems. Why waste energy on them? God knows, we need all we have!

Looking over the rehearsal schedule—backstage.

Two of ballet's greatest superstars were to be performing *Giselle* tonight at the Metropolitan Opera House. It just happened that I had the night off. Even more coincidental was the fact that one of the other dancers of the NYCB, who had planned on seeing the ballet, suddenly had to dance—so she offered me her ticket. There was only one problem, only one thing that prevented my going. Something I was ashamed to admit to her: *I didn't want to go!*

It was my only night off of the week. I didn't want to see any more dance. She scolded me and said that I should go and learn from watching. She is right. But what I really wanted to do was go see *Peter Pan*. It was playing on Broadway with Sandy Duncan.

"But you can see that any night!" she pressed on. It seemed she was determined to give me that ticket! "I know," I mumbled, "but I want to go tonight." She threw up her arms in exasperation, and I slithered out of the room. Really, I did want to see *Peter Pan*.

One of the most successful dauntless forms of beauty is talent. It can be overwhelmingly attractive. When *Peter Pan* was over, my heart was pounding and my palms were sweating. I was so excited that I had to go backstage and meet Sandy Duncan!

Fortunately, my father knows her well, so I had merely to mention his name to easily bypass the other fans. I met her. She was still in costume and makeup. We talked a bit, and I flattered her with the enthusiasm I felt. She, in turn, claimed to be envious of me in that I dance different ballets every night while she has been doing eight repeat performances a week for a year now.

I took my leave quickly so as not to overstay my welcome. I ran home. Now at twelve o'clock, I am still excited. It's madness. I would have been ready to spend the evening with her, doing whatever she wanted, believing anything she said.

However, I'll bet that two weeks hence I shall have completely forgotten about her. The thought of her will have a limited effect on my blood pressure. It's the talent that does it, I know. It's happened before.

It seems I am always falling in love with talent. This is worrisome. How can I ever be married and in love with one woman when I can be so easily bowled over in two hours by another!

When I was seven years old I was a rat. Balanchine had choreographed the three-act ballet *Don Quixote*, and in the opening section seven monsters charge through a mist to sword fight with Don Quixote. The smallest monster was the rat. Balanchine himself played Don Q. I'll never forget being terrified by the way Mr. B. battled us monsters. I had to use both hands and all of my seven-year-old strength to grip my sword because Mr. B. would have knocked it flying. He parried with such a tremendous, insane force I recall thinking, "That Don Quixote must have been a strong man."

When I was fourteen my mother took me to see *Man of La Mancha*. Richard Kiley was wonderful as Don Quixote. Afterward I remember feeling deeply sorry for the pitiful Don.

Only now after reading the book do I realize that what I felt all along was admiration. I think any man who knows anything about the character admires him. I would be him if I could. I would emulate him if I could. "The quest! The quest!" If I had my own quest, I would follow it as strongly as he. But where does one find a quest nowadays? I could almost believe that I could live for women. But it is not so. I could not live without them; neither could I live for them. I cannot live for dance either.

Even the lowest of men on earth can live nobly. Even they can die for a just cause. Where do I find a cause?

There are countless stories about pigheaded men who would not be dissuaded from carrying out some task with which they were obsessed. Their goal might have been the silliest and most childish, but they would not see reason. They would do what they must, no matter how stupid it might be. God, how I admire that—that ignorant pigheaded man who would not be swayed from his cockeyed notion!

I could never be that. I will always be swayed, always. Not by another, but by myself. There is always another side, another valid possibility.

Can one live for something different every day? How can one defend the principle of having no principles?

We are vitiated by indifference because we are pragmatic and opportunistic . . . We talk big and act small. We are so flexible, so elastic, that we can play any tune at all. And the more abstract our allegiances, the easier it is for us to evade responsibilities.

HENRY MILLER

The girls in this company always seem to be sewing their toe shoes.

I came down onto the stage to rehearse *Suite No. 3*. Since the rehearsal did not begin for ten minutes, I thought a little *tête-À-tête* with one of the girls would be more agreeable than warming up again.

They were sitting around the stage in small groups of twos and threes. Most of them were sewing shoes. Well, I suppose all these girls must learn to be prolific seamstresses; after all, they go through more than a pair of shoes a day. The NYCB shoe bill must be colossal!

Not feeling particularly invited to sit anywhere, I sat alone in the wings. No one would come and sit with me. I was not a part of those twos and threes. Back at Collegiate I was the gallant leader of an energetic host of scholastic musketeers, with a beautiful milady at my side, but that is all over now. I am sharply separated from them. And here I have no friends, no milady. That's what I need, a woman! Everything is wonderful when you have a woman with you. They are the fuel that makes me run. I am never more creative than when I am in love. And I have never been more intolerably inactive and pitiful as I am now without one. So I must find one here in the company. A wonderful woman to love and good friends are all one needs. I am certain of the woman I want. Sarah. She is perhaps the cutest girl in the company. She has no outstandingly beautiful features. In fact, separately her features are quite common, but collectively she is a total package of effervescent cuteness. The second I made up my mind to pursue Sarah I felt a familiar twinge of fear.

It must have been the devil himself who taught women those frightful words, that effective torture for all men: "Why can't we just be friends?" *Aaaaaaaaahhhhhhhhh!* God save me from this horrible fate; it has happened too often. Have I not had my share of suffering?

The first time was when I was fourteen. Up until then things had been exceptional.

When I did my last year of *The Nutcracker* I was thirteen. The other children of the cast were younger. I was the Nutcracker, the prince. Something about the role attracted all the girls, and I loved them all—one at a time. Sometimes I would even fall back in love with a previous one. We had something that we called our "order"—a numbered listing of our affections in rank of preference. The "order" changed practically daily. I rarely changed my mind. Cathy was always my favorite. However, I was not so thoughtless as to ignore the other girls who had me listed as number one in their "order." What a happy young boy I was, being carried around by the girls, literally carried. There were three girls in particular. Cathy I have already mentioned. Then there was Georgia with the large nose, and finally Maria, a Spanish girl with the kind of face that you knew would grow from cute to beautiful to stunning. In between matinee and evening performances of *The Nutcracker*, we would hang around the theater. One afternoon, I sneaked these three girls into my father's dressing room. He was not there. We had the place to ourselves so that we could engage in what we called "seven minutes in heaven." This involved a touching of closed lips in a kiss, for exactly seven minutes. It was so exciting the minutes whizzed by while we breathed heavily through our noses.

First was Georgia. We went into the bathroom and crouched down by the sinks. She sat with her back up against the built-in cabinets beneath the sink. There was a curtain which we drew separating us from the remaining girls who were sitting at the makeup mirror. We turned out the lights and the two girls watched their glow-in-the-dark watches for the completion of seven minutes.

Next came Maria. We repeated the same process, but Maria was much pleasanter. It was something about the way she rested her arms around me.

Again seven minutes flew by and she went out through the curtain. Now was Cathy, my favorite. Beautifully blonde, Cathy was the most physically mature of the group and had definite mounds recognizable as breasts. I announced, very boldly, that the other girls should ignore their watches, that Cathy and I would stop only when we wanted. I asked Cathy if this was O.K. with her. She looked at the floor and said, "Yeah." We closed the curtain.

Well, I knew what I wanted to do. I had been thinking about it all week. Now the thought of it terrified me. After about ten minutes of "heaven" I started my left hand moving. I pulled it off her back and worked my way to her belly. This took fifteen minutes. Really, I moved slower than a snail could possibly move. I moved at the rate of the minute hand on the clock.

I started my hand upward. Slowly it crept along. Oh, how my arm got tired from holding it up. You see, I hardly touched her, just the very lightest contact possible. Finally, I reached her little breast. Oh, my heart pounded! I could hardly breathe, and my breaths were coming out in little shivers. I was touching her so slightly that I didn't really feel anything, the excitement was that my hand was there. All this time Cathy had not moved. I wondered if she even knew what I had done. She must have. She offered no resistance. Then, I stopped and ended it. That was that. It was like reaching the time limit and stopping without thought. I had been very bold, but it was all right.

For the rest of the season every girl wanted to know if I had really done "you know" to Cathy. She must have told them, but they didn't believe her. I don't recall what response I gave them. Since then I don't believe physical contact has ever been that exciting. I reached the high point of my life at thirteen! My temple of gold. From now on I fear it may be downhill.

JULY

After four years as the Little Prince in Nutcracker, *I dance the Cavalier for the first time. Judith Fugate is the Sugar Plum Fairy.*

On closing night two men threw flowers onto the stage from the edges of the first ring which overlook the stage. The dancers in Balanchine's ballet to Bizet's *Symphony in C* stood on stage smiling, bowing, and ducking the small bouquets of roses. I stood in the wings watching. With the fall of the final curtain the female dancers each picked up a bouquet of flowers as they left the stage. Most of the women had already packed up their theater cases and would be changing out of their costumes and going home. Most of the men, myself included, had left their theater cases for the last minute and after the performance, at 10:30, had to start packing. From 10:30 to 11 the boys' dressing room was a spectacle of bare bottoms bent over black theater cases. I have no patience for folding clothes, so I just tossed all my things into the case, spread my makeup throughout the clothes so it would be cushioned, and before closing my bag, I carefully wrapped my worry beads in a wool leg warmer and placed it on top.

The next morning the stagehands picked up the cases, loaded them onto a truck, drove about four hours, and unloaded them again in the theater in Saratoga Springs, New York. The following morning we arrived. I pulled everything back out of the case and hung my beads from another makeup place. The dressing room was about the same size as in the New York State Theater, and so was the studio. In fact, just about everything was the same except the stage. The stage was outdoors. Beyond the last row of orchestra seats was a lawn on which people picnicked during performances. The Saratoga Performing Arts Center is called our summer home because we perform there each July. The rest of the summer the theater houses a variety of entertainments from the Doobie Brothers to Bob Hope.

Next to Skidmore College is a cluster of little apartments that are rented during the school year to students. My parents and I rented one of these. All the apartments are identical—square, sterile constructions with all the necessities for living. My parents rented a car because the theater is a few miles from the college. Since my father's and my schedules differed I often had to take the bus to the theater.

Despite the change in scenery everything carried on just as it did in New York. For some reason I thought that there would be big differences. I was excited to come here, but was quickly disappointed.

Why do I lose inspiration every time the alarm clock goes off? When early morning sunshine proposes sweating through another day at the theater, I don't radiate enthusiasm. Slowly I slide out of the bed onto the floor. From there it's not too far to the coffee pot. On many mornings, I forget the coffee and just rest in bed for "a few minutes." Unfortunately, the passing of minutes or hours is difficult to distinguish when one falls back to sleep. So on those mornings I miss class. My parents leave me totally alone, which is a blessing.

I wonder if my desire to dance is strong enough. Shouldn't I be thrilled to get up and rush off to the theater? I'm always glad when I do get up. Once I hit the morning air, it replenishes and exhilarates me. It is always a more successful day when it has begun early. Nonetheless, I often remain in bed.

Sometimes it's so hard to overlook instant gratification for that long-term satisfaction.

Alex slipped and sprained his foot this afternoon. No sooner had the news circulated when it was followed by the anxious tittering of a fearful question: Who would have to replace Alex in *Coppélia?*

Midway through the third act of Balanchine's *Coppélia*, the stage suddenly grows dark, and the music becomes ominous. Eight boys leap out of the wings dressed in Viking style, sporting silver spears and helmets and long blue capes. They dance a short and surprisingly tiring dance. Then again they hoist up their spears and exit, leaping off stage as they had entered. This section is called "War," and somebody had to replace Alex.

"Well, it better not be me," piped up Daniel. He sits at the end of the dressing room, and is always complaining. He pops hundreds of Hershey's chocolate Kisses into his mouth. In spite of all the sweetness that goes in only sourness comes out. Billy, at the other end of the dressing room, had a similar apprehension: "I always have to fill in for people. I bet I'll have to do it again!"

Sandwiched between these bickering boys were Luke and I, eating our lunch. We both had only one hour off. We had run to the deli, I returning with a tuna sandwich and Luke with roast beef. "How come you're not worried about having to fill in?" I asked Luke.

He smiled. "There's no way that I'll have to dance for Alex!"

"You seem sure of yourself. Why? Did you make a deal with somebody?" I chided him.

He just turned back to his sandwich. Daniel, who had overheard, yelled, "Of course he won't go in for Alex—he's already in it!" Luke let loose his slow cackle of a laugh.

"What's so funny?"

He looked up at me grinning. "*You're* going to have to do it."

"No way," I cried, and then threw my sandwich at him.

During a rehearsal, Rosie came up to me and hit me with the bad news. "No!" I screamed (to myself).

To her I said, "O.K."

Luke laughed hard when I told him.

"It's not funny," I insisted. "I had the whole weekend free!"

Luke just chuckled. I was really irritated.

In a few hours I was reluctantly putting on makeup. Then I went down on stage and began warming up.

Slowly something dawned on me as I mechanically did my *tendus:* I was glad to be doing "War"! In fact, I was looking forward to it. Here I was getting a chance to be on stage, to practice jumps, turns, to perform. I was lucky to be filling in for Alex! This realization made me wonder why I had reacted so vehemently against it this afternoon. It happened without my thinking. All day I had been hearing Daniel and Billy bitch about how awful it would be. Naturally, I adopted their opinion without my own thought. How foolish. All night I had been cranky and whining. If I had stopped to think for myself, I would have realized my excitement.

One has to be on guard all the time or else the miserable people will make you believe that you're miserable too. How easily things get twisted!

Feeling reinspired, I lined up with the boys awaiting our entrance. I stood right behind Luke. He was very serious, as we waited in the back wing. I like that about him. No matter what role he is doing, no matter how trite, he always tries very seriously and professionally. While others might be marking, or half-dancing, half-giggling with people in the wings, Luke would be dancing proudly. He inspired me. I imagined someone in the audience being particularly impressed with both Luke and me flying triumphantly through the air.

We all lined up in the back wing behind the ropes (in the third act there are several thick ropes that hang from the ceiling and drape out into the wing). "Five, six, seven, eight" and we were off! I started a little late but caught up directly. Halfway through we slammed our spears downward into the floor, and stood there while the girls entered. My feet were cramping awfully! I swear, I might point my feet for an hour in a rehearsal, but thirty seconds on stage and they cramp.

But there was no time to feel pain, for we were off again, jumping a circle around the girls, with our spears pointed high above our heads. Luke and I were jumping the highest. I wished Mr. B. or Jerry Robbins had been there to see us. But the first wing was empty so they had not come.

Suddenly, as Luke rounded the corner ahead of me, his spear caught in the ropes above his head! It all happened without his being aware, so he continued forward unknowing, the spear was wrenched from his hand and hung there in the ropes.

"*Ahhhhhhhh!*" he yelled, looking back. But he couldn't stop, he continued around the circle. Even if Mr. B. had been there, I would not have been able to control my hysterics. I laughed so hard, unable to arrest it. Neither could Luke. We had to stand on the side and pose for three eights. I stood with my spear up in the air, Luke stood holding up his empty hand. He pointed his finger upward as if that would help. We were both bouncing violently from our laughter.

Out of the corner of my eye I saw his spear untangle itself from the ropes, then fall loudly to the stage.

"Luke," I managed to say to him through my hysterics, "when we circle around again, pick it up!"

"O.K.," he cracked.

I think he felt relieved that he would soon be retrieving his spear. After the three eights, we circled around again. Luke had his eye on the fallen spear. As we rounded the corner, I saw a long wire slide out across the floor. It came from the wing closest to the spear. One of the stagehands was trying to get it off stage! I suppose he thought that someone might trip over it. Luke's face went white, and he panicked. He quickened his pace and lurched for the spear.

Just then the stagehand successfully hooked it and yanked it off the stage. Luke's hand brushed the end of it as he went by. Soon the stage manager was standing sternly in the wings yelling at us to stop laughing. But no

Making up.

way! Nothing could stop us. I tried, I really did. I had no idea what the audience thought, I suppose they noticed the dangling spear, they must have.

The minute we got off stage we received a heated lecture about our unprofessionalism. "But, if you could have seen his face!" I explained.

Dancers are often criticized for being conceited and vain. "They are always looking in the mirror, concerned with their bodies." This is only partially true. Certainly dancers are concerned with their bodies, but then so is any serious athlete. The difference is that the fastest runner wins the race, not the most beautiful one or the most graceful. There is no value put on *how* he runs. With the athlete it is merely a physical achievement. The dancer must combine physical prowess with a performance, with beauty, drama, all in relation to music. Every proportion of a dancer's body is important; not so with the athlete. The dancer is an artist. His body is the tool with which he works. So just as a violinist polishes and keeps his violin in good repair, or the sculptor looks after his tools, the dancer cares for his instrument—his body. When the violinist keeps a constant eye on his violin, no one accuses him of vanity; no one calls his preoccupation with the bow narcissism. But it happens that the dancer's tool and his own body are one and the same, so often his care of it is misunderstood. Dancers often look in the mirror to see what's wrong, what needs to be corrected. Of course, there are those who are vain and who find their reflection appealing. But what is universally felt by dancers toward their bodies is the same as the violinist to his instrument—pride. Pride, the sense of what one is worth, a natural self-respect.

I feel great sympathy for children who go to a school where one of their parents is a teacher. Any day the boy might be reprimanded—as all children are—for not do-

Linda Roy, Susan Freeman, and Helene Alexopoulous—waiting in the wings.

ing his homework or scoring badly on a test. But this one poor child is susceptible to the same reprobation on returning home at night! While other students are fibbing to their parents about their fine school day, this boy may not use deception for defense. If the student is a chronically lazy one, then he feels enough guilt without the teacher at home to increase it.

Well, it's just the same, you see, with my father. Every day I see him, and more awfully, he sees me! If I miss a company class, at night over dinner he asks, "So why'd you miss class?"

He does not reprimand me, but even if he did not mention it at all, his knowledge alone confronts me and gnaws at the guilt.

My father's constant presence aggravates an already festering sore. It is awful, but sometimes I wish he would go away. I almost hope that he won't be able to dance and then will not be around so much. What a selfish thought. I love him dearly and enjoy no man's dancing as much as his. But frequently these thoughts cross my mind anyway. What can I do? Unfortunately, we cannot regulate our thoughts as we can our actions.

The thing I truly need (besides a girlfriend) is to find my own apartment. That might solve the problem, but apartments are quite difficult to come by. There are several available down in the Village, or over on the East Side, but I want something close to Lincoln Center— some place I can walk to and from the theater, some place to dash to during an hour break. Some address close to my parents so that I can easily bring my laundry home!

There is something about Cynthia that disturbs me. I had been sitting on stage watching her rehearse. She was the only one of the ten girls who was not covered in leg warmers and she danced with full effort. I tried to evaluate her objectively. She has a lovely dancer's body—five feet nine inches or so, and most of her inches are legs. She always keeps her blond hair in a small bun tight on her head. A short upturned nose is her only facial feature that is not sharp and birdlike. Her physical attributes are more than adequate for a leading dancer. In addition, she is extremely intelligent with a well-rounded education and a quickness of wit. I am also aware, from past observances, that her talent and intelligence shine through and compliment her stage performances. Observing these facts one would conclude that Cynthia was bound to succeed. However, despite all her attributes, I know she will never make it. She will remain in the corps until she stops dancing.

How do I know? There is no visible fault, I just KNOW. I sense it somehow. I am unable to single out a reason for my prediction, it has something to do with the way she

Rehearsing with Jacques.

works. Although she works hard, it is a stagnant sort of labor. For example, she can kick her long legs as high as anyone, yet she does not control them on the way down. She allows gravity to recoil her leg. Every day in class she labors at flinging up her legs but never on controlling their descent. So it doesn't matter how hard she works—there will be no improvement. This sort of incomplete practice permeates all her dancing. The baffling thing is that she does not see it herself. She will plow onward painstakingly and see no improvement. I believe she will always be frustrated in the corps, and always keenly aware of her talent.

I sat watching her, feeling sorry and scared for her. She is nineteen. I wanted to warn her, "Quick, get out of here, go and do something else because you will have an unhappy life here." I cannot explain how I was so certain, but watching her, it seemed obvious. This was extremely unsettling for how do I know that I am not doomed to the same fate? I don't know it. Unfortunately, I cannot regard myself with the same unbiased clarity with which I can see others. Perhaps someone is looking at me and predicting the same fate.

Things get twisted so easily. Recently I find the most enjoyable part of the day is the end of it when I can return home and sit in bed with my feet propped up and a six-pack of beer in my lap. It is interesting to sit, absolutely still, in silence, in darkness, and slowly get drunk. I observe myself as the alcohol takes effect. However, I do not move about, so there is no clumsiness; my vision does not blur because it is pitch black; I hear no sounds; there are none of the common signs of drunkenness. After the six beers the only difference I notice is a heaviness about my body, as if a thick blanket had been placed over me, and my thoughts become lethargic. Each morning I am disgusted at the sight of six empty bottles; each night I open six more.

Ale, man, ale's the stuff to drink
For fellow whom it hurts to think

A. E. HOUSMAN

Next month we are off to Copenhagen. This will be my first European tour with the company. I have heard that the Danish have some of the best beer in the world!

What should we do when our sympathies conflict with our convictions? When we have told ourselves to act one way, yet we feel like acting otherwise? I always give in to the sympathies. It seems more natural, closer to "living the moment," which everyone claims is the ideal way to live.

Another choice is to force oneself to act upon premeditated rules, ignoring the present sympathies. That way seems so false. If we always felt the same about things, then a conviction should be acknowledged. But our convictions can change as often as our moods.

Indulging in spontaneity is one of the joys in life; an uncontrolled burst of desire. To me, there is nothing more enjoyable than riding blindly with one's immediate desires. Some people always wish to feel in control. They stifle their whims, overriding them with strict adherence to convictions. They feel good that they can be strong with themselves. I don't know how much they gain by living this way. It's like eating dinner at six o'clock, even though you are not hungry, just because you had planned to eat at that hour.

One thing I have learned is that simple pleasures are by far the finest. Why should people deny themselves one of life's natural pleasures?

The *tendu* is one of the first movements a dancer learns. It seems simple when observed. One leg moves forward from the fifth position. It extends outward with the foot pointing at the end. Then it returns to the fifth position. The *tendu* goes to the side and in back also. I watched Merrill Ashley as she warmed up for performance. The first ballet was already in progress. Merrill wasn't on until the last ballet. I too had come down to the stage to do a barre, but having no energy I sat and watched Merrill. I figured that watching her would inspire me to do my own warm-up. I began absentmindedly to count her *tendus*. She had done sixteen front before going side. Sparked by sudden curiosity I grabbed a pad and pencil and calculated—I must do over 10,000 *tendus* a year! I don't even work very hard! Imagine how many Merrill does! And that's just one exercise! Yet, here she is doing it again. She can never stop. Every day she does the same movements. She is never going to GET THERE; she'll never FINISH *tendu*. *Tendu* is not a goal that can be reached; one must always keep the coals burning, as it were.

Merrill is a principal dancer. I suppose we all wish to be on her level someday, but I don't know if I want to work that hard. Do I want to be doing *tendus* all my life? It seems so futile. You work and work at something relentlessly, you improve, certainly, but you never reach any finality. You just work until your body will no longer allow you. And there you are, and what can you show for it, not even *tendu* front!

If I could change one thing about myself I would change the fact that I care so much about what other people think of me. What value is the diffidence based on others' opinions? I find myself spending more time giving good impressions than I spend fulfilling my own desires.

My worst fault is that I would always give folks their own ways if it didn't seriously inconvenience me; I am too cowardly to refuse.

D. H. LAWRENCE

AUGUST

I now lead the Lennox regiment and have the pleasure of dancing with Jacques.

It's a very impressive sight—all the dancers sitting in the Kennedy Airport lounge waiting to board the plane for Copenhagen. We very rarely see each other in full street dress as we are mostly in leotards and the ever-popular plastic sweat pants. So now everyone is given an opportunity to impress their individual style upon the rest. The gossip mongers revel in these moments, for much is revealed. Pete might be carrying Linda's bags. *Bingo!* There begins a rumor! Jeff asks for a window seat for Elise, and the seat next to her for himself. *Bingo!* I'm sitting with Luke. I wonder if they'll start a rumor about that. The rumor mongers are the worst sort of gossips. They are dancers who don't find dancing, in itself, satisfying. It is not enough to occupy them; they are not content merely working. So they seek out and revel in debasing actions of everyone else. I suppose their self-esteem is heightened by depluming others. They are dangerous because they can suck you in very easily. There is something appealing about gossips. Like the sirens singing to Odysseus, they tempt one. To avoid them one must follow Odysseus' advice to his men: plug up the ears, and pass quickly by.

These gossips have a field day with me because I flirt with everyone! Is there harm in a flirt? Apparently so. Nasty Beth told me once at a party that she was disgusted at the way I treat women. This was astounding and I asked her why, to which she replied, "I know about the way you use women. I mean just offhand I could name seven of the dancers with whom you've indulged!"

I was appalled. I told her, "You had better not be seen talking with me, or else your name will be the eighth!"

Indeed she left. If I could only live up to my reputation, I would be a happy man.

After the take-off when the fasten-seat-belt sign was turned off, I stretched my legs with a walk toward the back of the plane. NYCB occupied almost half of the 747. On either side of the aisle dancers were chattering, giggling, sleeping. My father was not on the plane, for none of the ballets he dances are scheduled in Copenhagen. I had to carefully step over Suzanne Farrell who had stretched herself out in the aisle. The seats were too cramped for her long legs. I easily passed over her, but the stewardess, who was behind me, was less dexterous. She stopped at Suzanne's feet. "I'm sorry but you cannot lie there," she called out to Sue who, being asleep, did not respond. The indignant stewardess bent over to wake her up. "Don't wake her up!" cried one of the dancers. The stewardess explained, "She cannot block the aisle." "Oh, let her sleep," called another dancer from the opposite end of the plane. "Yes, let her," joined in two other dancers. Soon the poor stewardess was receiving pleas from all around, and so great were the number of voices that she mumbled under her breath and passed over Sue, leaving her to sleep. As she went by I thought I saw a faint smile appear on Suzanne's face. There is a feeling of courage that one gets when he holds the majority. I felt very confident, a cocksureness that blooms from a feeling of security.

This same feeling prevailed as we rode the bus into Copenhagen from the airport. Everyone wanted to be the first to see something of novelty, and we all yelled out each discovery as quickly as we could, while the small Danish contingency smirked condescendingly. We were now in Copenhagen! Almost all of the dancers were staying in the same hotel. The switchboards were furiously busy all night with requests from dancers to know their friends' room numbers. A great deal of comradery seems to grow between the company members when we go on tour. The feeling of being a unit, a family, increases the farther we get from home. I was glad of this. I wish it would grow even stronger.

The day we arrived in Copenhagen was sunny and glorious. Unfortunately, every day afterward was overcast, cold, and rainy. One night Luke suggested we go out looking for Danish women. We both heard of how Copenhagen held an abundancy of them—all blond, blue-eyed, and well proportioned. Naturally, I was willing. But picking up girls was something I had never attempted.

"What should I wear?" I asked him. I sounded like a schoolgirl going out on a first date.

"Oh, don't be silly, it doesn't matter."

I could see that it didn't. Luke was wearing a green-and-yellow-plaid jacket, and maroon pants.

"O.K.," I said, grabbing my hat and the hotel key. Somehow I couldn't imagine us having any success.

"Sure we will," he assured me. "The foreigners love Americans. You've just got to know how to approach them."

We stalked down the "walking street," which was a tourist center, a mile-long street, on which cars were prohibited. All along the way were stores, selling everything from pipes to Levi's. A constant flux of young women paraded up and down the street. Many were beautiful, but all of them had an equally or even more beautiful man escorting them. Suddenly the futility of our situation occurred to me.

"Luke, how can we ever meet anyone? Do you speak Danish?"

"Don't be thick," he scolded. "This is Europe—everyone speaks English!"

We walked on awhile in silence. Way ahead of us I spotted a pair of well-fitted Levi's, blond-locks, and a blue-and-white-striped shirt. The stripes were impressively stretched and distorted by the woman's filling. Before I could share my news with Luke, he was already heading toward her. He walked boldly, self-assured.

I was very impressed with his confidence. I quickly caught up to him, but trailed slightly behind. I didn't want to speak the first words. What could I say? "Hi, I'm with the New York City Ballet. We're dancing over at Tivoli. Do you want to go out for a drink?" Not so good. So I left it up to Luke.

He stopped in front of her. "Excuse me," he said. She stopped to listen. Luke raised his left arm, turning his wrist as if to look at his watch. His right hand pointed to where his watch would be, if he had one. "Can I see your tits?" he asked her calmly. I lost all control. Howling with laughter, I had to turn around and double over in convulsion.

"Yes." She smiled at him, and looking at her watch answered, "Forty-five minutes after nine."

He thanked her and moved on down the street. For the rest of the night we raced from girl to girl. Whoever met her first asked the question, while the other giggled behind. When one woman told us that it was 11:45 we decided it was time to sleep, so we returned back to the hotel feeling exhilarated and wonderfully childish.

The dressing rooms in Copenhagen are not quite as modern as those in New York. Here the entire men's corps inhabits a few small rooms with small tables and small mirrors. There is difficulty in correctly judging the shade of makeup in the insufficient lighting of these rooms. I don't even have my own makeup place, but since I don't dance here anyway, that is justified.

I wish I did dance here, particularly at night during performances. Often I sit out in the front of the theater as part of the audience. I am proud of the company's performances, but I don't feel quite justified in this pride. I am not contributing. The Danish are thrilled with our ballets, they probably will ask us to return next year. Perhaps when we do return, I won't feel like the "water boy." The "water boy" was a title we gave the high school basketball team's errand boy. Even worse than the "water boys" were the "scrubs"! These were the lesser members of the team. These disappointed lads sat carefully at the end of the bench during a game. They would await an opportunity to see some playing time. The coach put them in only when the team was way ahead, or hopelessly behind. The "scrubs" spent each game trying to keep their legs moving and warm "just in case." We also called them "bench warmers."

I never dreamed, when I quit the basketball team in tenth grade, that I would ever have to consider the possibility of being a "scrub." But that seems to be my status here in Copenhagen. Tonight I was sitting in the dressing room warming the chair of another dancer who was out on stage.

Luke was putting on his makeup for *Episodes*. That's the only solo he does. I sat with him killing time during intermission. I noticed something peculiar about Luke. He sat bare-chested, his alabaster-tone skin almost glowed in contrast to his jet-black hair. But on his chest was one hair, just one, dead center, perfectly aligned above his bellybutton. This was no ordinary chest hair. It coiled like a spring tight against him and it looked as if, when pulled straight, it would stretch five inches! I sat in amusement, estimating the length of the singular hair, when some extraordinary commotion occurred outside the dressing room.

Actually it was the opposite of a commotion; all had become suddenly silent. Luke and I were startled at this peculiar phenomenon. We looked at each other. In silent unison we arose from our seats and entered the hall. The hall was filled with the male dancers all standing in a group, all absolutely silent. I feared someone was hurt. Perhaps there had been an accident. But the feeling about this cluster suggested another explanation. I forced my way into the crowd. Everyone was looking out one window. What could be so fascinating about a window that overlooked a courtyard? It was a tiny square courtyard which I believed was inaccessible. Who could be there? When I reached a view from the window I discovered the reason for this gathering. Directly across from us one floor below was the girls' dressing room. Less than twenty feet opposite us was a widely opened window. Sitting at the open window was Jasmine. Oh, how lucky that it was Jasmine! She is an older dancer. It is unanimously agreed that she is one of the sexiest. She had a perfectly proportioned body—slim long legs and wonderfully rounded breasts.

Having just finished dancing *The Four Temperaments*, she was wearing only tights and a black leotard. I, too, became breathless, knowing that she might at any moment remove those two slight pieces of clothing. We all hoped desperately that she would not notice us, at least not until the deed was done.

After she pulled the last pin from her long black hair, she stood up and pulled at the left strap of her leotard. For that one second there was not a heart in the hall that did not skip. Turning around she pulled down the leotard, and her naked back was revealed to us. Our breathing increased. I was nudged slightly to the side by Dennis. I looked at him for a second in wonder. He is gay yet seemed as intensely interested as I. I returned my full attention to the window. Jasmine was tossing her tights into her theater case. She turned and walked back to the mirror. There she was, standing less than twenty feet away, absolutely naked, combing her hair. It was all so perfect that I couldn't believe she was truly oblivious to us. Perhaps she was giving us a show! She continued to brush her hair as I left the window. To my surprise she wasn't as exciting as I had anticipated. I was actually disappointed with her nakedness. The most exciting part was the anticipation.

Soon screams were heard as the girls discovered the intrusion. The window was slammed shut.

The girls were indignant for a week.

There is something about going on tour that makes many of the dancers frisky. Late-night room swapping is quite frequent. It might be due to a feeling of freedom that comes with being away from home, or maybe there is just a greater longing for companionship on tour. One night I saw one of the male dancers enter a girl's room at three in the morning but then come down for breakfast with a different girl!

It is possible that this sort of entertainment occurs with equal frequency in New York City. But if so, it's not as noticeable as it is here. Most of us are staying in the same hotel and it's quite difficult to keep secrets.

Almost every night there is a party given in the company's honor. Glorious buffets of Danish cuisine are ours to devour, after we have listened to the host's loquacious praise of Balanchine. Luke and I are among the last to leave these parties; they always serve Carlsberg and Tuborg, the renowned Danish beers. The real reason I stay so late is the dancing. These Danish bands play terrific Duke Ellington jazz. This is the kind of music I like dancing to. None of this disco dancing, although I've done my share of it in New York where there are the grandest disco palaces in the world. Disco is so limited that I quickly lose interest. One is forced to move within the framework of a very strong pounding beat. There is little room for variety. On the other hand, ballroom dancing involves countless possibilities. One can even use steps from ballets and jazz them up a bit to make them unrecognizable. I like dancing *with* my partner. In discos one generally loses one's partner altogether upon reaching the dance floor. It always makes me laugh to see a boy shyly ask a blushing girl to the disco floor. Once on the floor they totally ignore each other and dance off into their own worlds. When the song ends they struggle through the crowd to find each other and decide if they wish to dance to the next song. Ballroom dancing—that's the romantic stuff!

These Copenhagen bands are ideal. I dance all night long, changing partners with each song. A ballerina's vocal cords can hardly produce sweeter sounds than, "I thought you were going to dance with me this time!"

All of the slow romantic waltzes I save only for Sarah. She is always willing, so it encourages me that perhaps she is not totally indifferent to me. She doesn't stay at these parties quite as long as I. Since I am not performing here in Copenhagen, I don't have to worry about getting up early for company class. I think the company only brought me here in case someone is injured.

It was audition day for Jerry Robbins. Danny Duell was out with a bad back, and someone would have to dance the "Spring" section of *Four Seasons* for him. Three boys were called: Jeff, Simon, and myself. The ballet wasn't scheduled to be performed until November, but Jerry wanted to be certain of a suitable replacement. Danny would be out for six months. I felt flattered to be called to this rehearsal, but the memory of my previous rehearsal with Jerry made me apprehensive. It was reassuring, at least, to know that this time there were two other boys besides me.

The rehearsal began without Jerry. He had telephoned that he would be a little late. Sara Leland, a principal dancer who also acts as an assistant, took the rehearsal. She is one of the few people who seems to have even greater energy than I. She asked us to begin with the *pas de deux*. "I don't know who Jerry wants to do this. I don't think he knows yet." She explained to us, "So, Jeff, why don't you work with Judy (Judy was the alternate for the girl's part), and Simon, I'll work with you. Chris, there is no one for you to work with, so just try to follow."

I was relieved not to have a partner. Both Jeff and Simon are six feet tall and twenty-four years old. Being lesser in both age and height, I felt lesser in ability, too.

After a half hour, Jerry walked into the studio. He faced us, rubbed his hands together, and told us to start with the boys' variation. I nonchalantly positioned myself behind Simon and Jeff.

Jerry taught us the variation. Here I had an advantage over the others; I was already in the corps of "Spring" and had seen the variation countless times. I used to dance it backstage during performance. Naturally, I kept this to myself and acted totally ignorant. Once everyone had learned it, Jerry had us run it through. In preference to dancing alone, all three of us danced it together, often bumping into one another. It was not a simple variation. Following along backstage was easy enough, but here in the studio I could hardly complete it! I was reassured by the fact that neither Jeff nor Simon could get through it either. Jerry let us catch our breaths before commanding that we do it one at a time starting with Simon.

Simon gathered his strength and courage before attempting the piece. As Simon was struggling through the steps, it occurred to me that I had a great advantage over them both. They would spend most of their energy worrying about getting the steps right and staying with the music, while I, previously familiar with the ballet, needed only to concentrate on dancing well.

Simon finished the variation a little late and very dizzy. Jerry beckoned for Jeff to go next. Jeff took a deep breath and started. I stood shaking on the side. It was like waiting in the doctor's office to get a shot—waiting with affected calm for something you know is going to hurt. I looked at Simon, who was leaning over the barre breathing hard and wished that I could have been him right then.

Jeff, beaten and puffing, passed by me, as I walked to the back of the studio to begin. I didn't look at Jerry or in the mirror. I looked down at the floor. The introduction went by, and I flung myself into the first leap. Then something happened. Halfway through I felt as though I had stepped out of my body and hovered, whispering in my ear, "Good! You're doing great!" I thought to myself, "Whatever it is that we try to achieve by daily toil, today I've got it!" I finished the variation with my stomach cramped from exhaustion, but it was a triumphant pain.

We worked on the variation piece by piece for the remainder of the rehearsal. All the while I had this incredible feeling that I could have done anything Jerry might demand. Eagerly, I stood at the front of the room, and always went first.

Jerry left us heaving for breath on the floor while he talked with Sara. He thanked us and left.

I picked myself off the floor and shuffled into the hall for a drink of water. Sara came up behind me with a big grin on her face. "You're on," she said.

"I'm on?" I gasped.

"Yep." She could not stop grinning. "You'd better get together with Judy and start rehearsing."

Sometimes dreams do come true. Sarah came to my room last night. There was no doubt of our intentions. We got started so quickly that I hardly had time to get nervous. The next morning when Sarah had left to take class, I ordered breakfast in bed and tried to find a reason why I had not enjoyed the evening. How could I not have had a good time? I did not wish to admit it, but halfway through the sex, I had found myself wishing she would leave! The major disappointment came right away. I didn't like the way she kissed. That sounds trivial, but it is the most important thing to me. Kissing is the finest thing a man and a woman can do together; it is the most exciting, most expressive, most satisfying of contacts. Unfortunately, it was obvious that kissing didn't matter to Sarah.

Ever since I can remember I have desired women. Physical beauty was the attraction; love was not important. With Sarah I felt, for the first time, that sex for its own sake was disappointing. Maybe my previous experiences were exciting because I was learning about sex. But last night it was a tedious effort. Perhaps it is true what they say—that sex without love is really not worthwhile.

The company takes bows—closing night in Copenhagen.

The return flight was not as exciting as the departure had been. Many of the dancers were tired of performing and sick of eating herring. We all looked forward to returning home. Even though I didn't perform at all on this tour, I finally felt as if I was really a part of the company. It was those terrific parties that did it!

When school friends are choosing sides for a basketball game and you get picked first—WOW! what a wonderful feeling. Likewise, being the last choice is misery. In Copenhagen I was first! I was—oh, dare I use the word—POPULAR! I fit into the groups now. I am part of those twos and threes. It's delightful to have friends who save you a place at the barre for class. Or who wonder, "Where is he?" if you don't show. Most of these friends are women; well, actually *all* of them are, except Luke.

Along with everything right there is always something wrong. The downfall of this tour was Sarah. Our relationship did not progress well. She came to my room two more times. I felt somehow obligated to invite her. I thought that perhaps if we continued things would improve. They did not. What I really wanted to do was to forget the whole thing, pretend it never happened. But that is not right. On the last night we talked. I think she already knew what I was feeling, and I don't think she minded terribly. "Why not? Why didn't she mind?" I thought, but was really relieved. And so we parted friends.

As I had previously observed, things could not be kept very secret in that hotel. It wasn't long before the news of Sarah's and my misadventure was in circulation.

"Good morning, Ellen."

"Good morning, Lisa. Beautiful day, isn't it?"

"Oh yes," Ellen replied. "I see you have the morning paper there. What's the news?"

"Well, let's have a look. The Russians have entered Afghanistan, there are earthquakes in Italy, bomb scares in Chicago, and Chris and Sarah slept together!"

The one person to actually approach me on the subject was Beth. She was merciless in reprimanding me. She knows well the sore spot to thrust her sword. I don't think I like her.

When a man throws all his money into one big gamble and loses, he will naturally be very upset. And people will console him by saying, "It's O.K. We all learn from our mistakes."

If he drinks too much at a party and plays the fool, he will be embarrassed the next morning. But his girlfriend will say, "Never mind, we learn from our mistakes."

So I made a mistake with Sarah. It was wrong. But a woman will not forgive a mistake involving another woman. Oh no. Beth will not tell me that I learned from this mistake. No, women will attack you as a criminal and tear at your heart with their accusations. "You *used* her," they cry. That's always it, isn't it?

Beth reparried her last thrust, leaving me crushed. I felt like standing and yelling out the whole saga to the passengers, then throwing myself at their feet for judgment.

"I plead guilty with extenuating circumstances. Forgive me, I made a mistake!"

SEPTEMBER

"Fall" section of Four Seasons.

When one gets on an airplane and flies away it is very exciting. It is as if life starts over for you. Everything is a novelty. There are new excitements as well as fresh new problems.

However, on the return trip the feelings are not as optimistic and fresh. Sitting in your room, hanging in the closet, lying in your bed are all those unsolved problems you thought were gone—but you merely neglected to fold them into your luggage. They remained behind unchanging—only collecting dust. And now you are returning to them with a suitcase full of new problems.

The biggest of them is a monster who lies in my head poking and nudging me as I sleep. This monster is the "Spring" section of the ballet *Four Seasons*.

One is supposed to be happy when getting to dance a leading role. But this ballet seems like some extremely advanced school exam that glares at me from six weeks away. I know I can never pass it. Perhaps in two years, yes, but not six weeks.

How ironic that I regret dancing well. I am sorry for having been so dexterous in that audition with Jerry. I fear he thinks me better than I really am. That rehearsal was just a fluke, an aberration. Either Jeff or Simon would be better for the part; they are more experienced and consistent.

It's not so much that I'm afraid, although that adds to the problem. If there were absolutely no one more qualified than I to do it, then all would be right, but that's not the case. . . .

I recently became attracted by the poetry of Lord Byron. I do not often read poetry because I do not often understand it, but Byron is simple and beautiful. Sparked by this interest, I went to see a play devoted to Byron and became instantly fascinated with his life. I also became acquainted with the actor who portrayed him.

In a dank, smelly old bookshop down in Greenwich Village, I laid my hands on the most impressive volume of

Byron I had ever seen. It was an 1876 edition of all his poems and his letters. It was an old, beautiful book with heavy brown binding and big gold letters impressed on the cover: BYRON. It looked almost like a Bible.

I clasped this book to my heart, while delivering the necessary bills from my pocket.

I brought this prize with me to my second viewing of the show. Afterward, I took it backstage to show to the actor. His eyes sparkled when he held it!

"I can't believe you found this in a bookstore!" he cried.

I felt very proud of my book. He thanked me for showing him and dashed off to a party. I took the book and reluctantly placed it on his makeup table—on the first page I wrote:

> *If someone had snatched up this book and bought it before me—only because he thought the binding attractive—I would have felt it an injustice—knowing how much more it would have meant to me. When I saw your reaction to it, this same injustice was there. I would have been a criminal to retain it. Therefore, I leave this treasure with you on the premise that should someone value it even more than you, you will relinquish it to him.*

It is this same sense of injustice that makes me uncomfortable about dancing "Spring." It should be for others who would do it better. At present, I am not the most qualified.

The most valuable thing I have learned from my father is the importance and worth of analyzing. It is a key to success in any field. He suggests always beginning at the simplest starting point, keeping the ultimate objective in sight, and searching for the most direct path to reach it. A straight line between two points.

"Always keep things simple," he advises. "Approach things as you would a geometry problem. Find the most effective method to achieve your goal. If you have common sense and the ability to analyze, then you can do anything, and do it well!"

It was in taking this idea literally that I formulated my equation on happiness:

$$\text{GOAL} + \text{ABILITY} \times \text{ENERGY} = \text{HAPPINESS}$$

However, I no longer believe this to be true. It is not a false equation but neither is it complete. There are countless flaws that can render this formula inadequate. A common deterrent is what I am suffering from. I have discovered it in myself, and I now see it everywhere. One needs the ability to convert *desire* into *deed*; the act of taking an idea from the head and making it real—completing it. A great many people suffer from the gift of spoken language. They use that outlet to vent their inspiration. Being temporarily calmed, they never follow through. They just talk and dream about their goals. Talking is dangerous for people who wish to accomplish. The dreaming and the telling of an idea will most certainly assuage the desire. It's like a leak in a steam engine through which small amounts of steam escape; the engine can never build up enough pressure to function.

From childhood we are programmed to revel in success and avoid failure. "Stick with what works and one should never fail." What a disillusioning philosophy! No one actually says, "Don't fail," but it is universally felt that one should avoid it at all costs. If we engage only in that which assures success, then our learning process dies, and all possible growth is stunted. The range of possible experience would be narrow and fixed. Soon what was previously only fear of failure becomes fear of change. People learn to cling to that which first proves successful. They will stick with it even though later it might be the cause of problems.

I'm sure everyone had a friend in childhood who had a particular "act," his own special quirk that made him popular with others. As time passes and the children mature, the boy who is still doing the same "bit" begins to lose his popularity. You now grow tired of him, having, yourself, grown out of that phase. Meanwhile, the boy is unhappy and doesn't know why. He concludes that the fault lies with the others since "he, himself, hasn't changed." So now more than ever he sticks to his act. What was previously working for him is now holding him back.

There is a perfect example of this here in the ballet. Andrew joined the company at a very young age. He was a talented youngster and excelled quickly. But now he is older and his advancement has slackened. What worked well for him as a child is not what will work for him as an adult. A change is required. One must continue to grow. He works hard but only in the same adolescent direction, so in the end he starts losing roles to someone younger than he, someone whose skill has already surpassed his. He cannot understand why and concludes that Balanchine holds a grudge against him. When we don't succeed it is natural to search for a reason, and it is always easier to find the fault with others than with ourselves. Andrew still tells the same jokes, and his dancing still has the same faults.

This same problem takes place in practical, everyday performing. When a dancer is given an opportunity to dance a principal role, he seeks to find out everything about how it was done before him, so that he can duplicate the performance. Most dancers shun originality, but Balanchine doesn't want to see a copy. He wants to see how *you* do his steps, not how you imitate your predecessor. One must put oneself completely into the role, and if Mr. B. doesn't like it, then too bad. But don't copy—a copy is never as good as the original. *You* want to be the original. Let your successor copy you.

One should keep in mind the philosophy of trying everything once. That way, one learns just what works and what doesn't. The human consciousness functions freest of apprehension when the elements of the world that affect it are safely filed away, so that one knows just what everything is and where it can be found.

It is lovely to return to the New York State Theater. Everything is exactly the same, like a home away from home. My first rehearsal of the day was for Balanchine's ballet *Brahms-Schoenberg Quartet*. I dance in the fourth movement, directly behind my father. He and Suzanne were rehearsing the *pas de deux* on stage when I arrived to rehearse. I sat and watched them. My father was being his usual exuberant self, while Sue coolly and introvertedly went through her steps.

It made me smile to know that when they perform the ballet, the roles will be practically reversed—Sue will be carrying on like a wild tramp while my father will try to be subdued.

"You have to be aware of what the girl is doing," he told me. "When Sue is carrying on, I try to play it cool. That way we balance each other. If I carried on as well, then together we would be too much. So I leave it to her, but if she decides to be subdued one night, then I'll spring forth with eagerness. It's very important that two dancers balance each other."

There was a sharp laugh from Rachael and a smaller giggle from Gwen. They were sitting near me sewing their shoes. It irritated me. Not that I dislike laughter, but Rachael does it all the time. She is always making the same jokes while her friend Gwen is always giggling at them. It becomes tiresome after a while; predictable. One is always entertaining while the other is always being entertained. Come to think of it, they also balance each other.

But I don't believe them. I don't believe their friendship. It's all surface involvement. They claim to be friends, but I don't believe they really care to know about each other. Oh, certainly Gwen knows how many brothers and sisters Rachael has and that her grandmother died last year. And Rachael knows that Gwen has two cats. But that's all they want to know.

How pitiful that seems; how false and pitiful.

I looked around the stage at all the people who claimed friendship. How many of them were real? How many? *None!* Not one! Among all the people in this rehearsal there is not one true friendship. What a disgusting statistic! What are they "friends" for? Why bother? . . . Oh, I have committed a terrible hypocrisy. *My* friends and I are no better! I am as guilty as everyone I condemn. My friendships are no deeper than that of Gwen and Rachael.

It happens without notice. One can condemn others without seeing the hypocrisy.

It is in our human nature that we all need companionship. But here we work so hard that there is no time for outside relationships. We *must* satisfy our natural needs with the few people here in the company. So what results are friendships of *necessity*, not *emotion*. Friends are made because friends are needed, not because someone is truly interested! There are only a few people in the whole company whose friendships of necessity grow into something greater. But only a few.

I don't think I want the kind of friendship that most everyone seems to offer here. I'd rather do without. I want a friend who will want to know more about me than I know about myself, and vice versa. I don't want just a human pastime. I can turn on the TV and get the same.

It is disappointing to realize these are friendships of necessity. I believed them winsome, so comforting. But they will never be that for me again, now that I have understood them. They are like a drug that makes you feel great while under the influence, but there is no real value. These friends work like an escape, like running off to a movie to avoid oneself. But that does not help anyone because then problems are never confronted, and no action is taken to resolve them. Then we end up like Andrew who never changes, who will shoot up with friendships of necessity when he is bored. No, I must kick this habit. I must separate myself from these specious pastimes.

Suzanne Farrell and Jacques in the last movement of Brahms-Schoenberg Quartet.

During a very long and boring *Coppelia* rehearsal rather than practice, I finished reading D. H. Lawrence's *Women in Love*. I now have read the book twice and seen the movie three times.

It is said that Lawrence created the character named Rupert Birkin after himself. Birkin's most amiable quality is that he is highly sensitive and blindly obedient to his own nature, or at least he tries to be. By his own nature, I mean those capricious impulses that are not consciously controlled; spontaneous whims. It is his indulging in spontaneity that I admire.

Spontaneity is most uplifting in situations where individuality is least expected. The more artificial the situation, the more welcome it is—sprouting from falseness, something real and unique appears.

It occurred to me that the same holds true for dancing. After all, ballet is one of the most artificial activities existing.

Of all the ballerinas I have seen, without a doubt Suzanne Farrell is the Queen of Spontaneity. She seems to be in total command of the stage, and one never sees two identical performances. She always takes advantage of her whims on stage.

Once she said to me, "I hardly ever do what I rehearse. I may not feel the same on stage as I did in rehearsal. It's taken me a long time to be able to dance that way."

It is this quality of her performance that makes me always eager to watch her. In this ability lies Suzanne's greatness.

Emily Calison was a woman of seventy-nine years. She died last week. I didn't know her. Apparently she had very little money, and all she left behind her was a vacant apartment on bustling Columbus Avenue, eight short blocks from Lincoln Center. This was not the most desirable circumstance under which to acquire an apartment, but in New York these days it takes a death to attain one. I leaped at the opportunity, having been informed of it by a dancer whose flat was catty-corner to the late Mrs. Calison's. The landlord was pleased with me, particularly because I paid him immediately. I returned directly home and packed up all the items to which I could claim any sort of ownership. With a final stealthy perusal of the kitchen I casually pilfered extra utensils that were duplicates and therefore might vanish unnoticed.

"Finally I can live alone!" I thought to myself. "I am really a man now, right?" On my first night in my new home I bought twenty red candles and a bottle of champagne. I perched all the candles randomly about the all-in-one living room, dining room, den—a rectangular room, it was otherwise severely vacant. On the floor in the bedroom lay a mattress and a pillow. In the kitchen I placed my culinary plunder; one brown coffee mug, one plate, one fork, and two corkscrews, neither of which was needed to open the champagne.

I popped the cork, filled the inappropriate mug, lit the candles, fitted my Sony earphones into place. I sang along with Bing Crosby—"You've got to *ac-cent-tchu-ate the positive.*" My voice, probably hideously out of key to another listener, sounded, to me, exactly like Bing's. I raised my cup, toasted the candles, and drank to this novel bachelor life.

If one is to separate oneself from others, to leave something behind, there must be another place to go. It is possible for people to wrap themselves in their dreams and their work. It is a form of hiding, but it can prove advantageous. That is where I shall go. However, there's another problem. It is the fault of scattered dreams—several intense desires all scattered in different directions. Some are much more important than others, but none are unimportant. The essence of the problem lies in the fact that never can one dream be approached before another appears demanding attention. There is little time to begin one before another is piquing the brain. Consequently, several things get started but nothing completed.

It's like having a hundred choices for dessert, and you hate to give up any, so you try to eat all of them and end up with a bellyache and one hundred half-eaten desserts. I need to limit myself to one pure, direct objective, only one obsession that is stronger than everything else and rich enough to satisfy this sweet tooth.

This is exactly what dancing should be for me. It is by far the strongest of my desires. But it is not strong enough to shield my mind from outside diversions. I used to be so proud of my outside interests, but now they are only a frustrating burden.

I have been in this company for six months, and for six months I have been only partially dancing. I have not done it right! I have let myself slip into a miserable state of inaction. Six months of riding the wave, but not swimming. It is time to stop talking and start doing. Stop dreaming and force desire into deed! That is the only way to learn. Take the chance. I am young and aging rapidly. Youth is the time for chances. I must now throw myself into dancing—up over my head without testing the water first. I have done enough testing. All strength, energy, and desire must be focused into one objective. I must push aside all other interests that will seek to dissuade. One hundred percent dance. No quitting! No holding back!

In order to be absolutely certain, I must give this effort a fair chance. So I write down and would sign in blood if that weren't obsolete:

Today, September 6, I begin. In one year, again on September 6 I will ask myself, "Is this right for me? Have I been happy this year?" If the answer is negative, then I must leave, maybe join my friends at college, a year late. If the answer be positive, then that is that.

I must be consistent during this year even if it is hateful work. It will be worth the misery to discover for certain what I want or at least, perhaps, what I don't want.

When one wishes to break a bad habit it is easier to succeed if a new habit is formed simultaneously. I am full of bad working habits, beginning with my habitual inattendance of morning class. In these last six months I must have slept through more classes than I attended. That will be the first habit broken, and if I fail in this, then the rest is doomed. How can one work on breaking bad working habits when one is not even working!

It is waking up in the mornings that is the difficulty. It takes a few minutes for ambition to fully wake up to take control, and those few minutes of weakness are just long enough for the powerful sandman to render me unconscious again.

I found a little gray plastic box in the hardware store. On the top is the face of a clock. This convenient machine is designed to discourage burglars by turning the lights in your house on and off while you are out of town. It can be set to activate the lights at any hour. Eight-thirty does fine for me. The lights miraculously illuminate at that hour of the morning and wreak havoc with my pupils. I now am awake long enough for ambition to surface while the lights keep the sandman hiding in the closet. By nine o'clock I have made it to the coffee shop, which is halfway to the theater. Following several cups of coffee I leave to soak in the Jacuzzi in the dressing room. By the time 10:30 class rolls around, I am limber and energized.

This little plastic box was invented in 1968. If I had been born twenty years ago I probably would have quit dancing.

I attempted to read a book by the philosopher Gurdjieff. I was promptly confused and bored. So I went directly to his disciple who I had heard was easier. I began

Tertium Organum by P. D. Ouspensky. The first sentence read: "The most difficult thing is to know what we do know, and what we don't know."

Well, that seemed simple enough, I immediately put the book down and went around the corner to the stationery store and bought the biggest pad of lined paper I could find. Returning to my apartment with this large pad and thick pen I placed it on my desk and wrote at the top "What I Know." I planned to leave this pad and pen there for a week and every time I thought of something I knew, I would add it to the list. I sat and began the list. I wanted to start at the beginning, the simplest way. To my astonishment this list was commenced and completed in only ten minutes. I began:

I know that I exist.
I do not know how I exist or why.
I know of other people and objects in relation to myself, only through my five senses.
I don't know how my senses exist or what they really are. Therefore, I cannot be sure of anything that my senses report.
I know nothing.

That was it. What a waste of paper! I picked up the book again just to read the same conclusion I had drawn. Then, of course, the book went on to discuss time and space, dimensions, perceptions, etc.

I was most excited at my own discovery of what probably would have meant little to me had I let Ouspensky tell me. The point was that I had thought of it for myself, and it remained with me long after the book was forgotten. I had learned something that I understood and believed.

Since I am to be devoting myself for the next year to dancing, it seems logical to approach dancing the same way I did Ouspensky. Starting from the beginning; even before the beginning. Starting with nothing and make the beginning. Much of my knowledge of dance has been given to me. And I have accepted it without question, perhaps without complete understanding. If someone were to ask me to explain why I believe *rond de jambe* should outline a circle with the leg rather than a half circle, which is commonly taught, I would have no understanding outside of that I know it should be done. I know it's right. There is very little strength in belief without understanding.

I must approach dancing from scratch and find my own conclusions. We all tend to allow the doctrine that because something is universally believed it must be true—or cannot bear improvement. However, there are always a few who search and discover new truths, and we say, "Oh yes! You are right! How obvious. Why didn't we see it sooner?"

In order to be open-minded I must strip all the predetermined responses, throw away all youthful programming, shuck off all that is known, all that has been taught, and learn like a child again. But this time being taught only by the facts and truths, not by tradition, or customs.

But now what? Now that I have successfully gotten myself consistently into class, I must work on improving technique.

If one is truly to start at the beginning, the first thing to do is to inspect the equipment. Make sure all the necessary proportions are adaquate. *Aaaahhhhh* the FEET! THE FEET! My father never had a good arch; my mother never had an adequate *pointe*. If you take the genes of separately inadequate feet, and produce another pair . . . guess what? My feet don't point!

Perhaps I should not start quite so efficiently. Maybe I should overlook the equipment check. No. If I begin with compromises then I am doomed to mediocrity.

So the feet are not good enough—I must make them better!

The first thing to do is to get a pair of toe shoes. The best way to stretch and strengthen the feet would be to exercise in those rock-hard shoes that the women wear.

I purchased a pair of size 9EEE. They were black, and less noticeable than pink ones. It was my resolution to exercise five minutes immediately after every class. This is the ideal time because I'll be warmed up but not exhausted. At the end of class all the dancers are standing around or working on steps and it is quite embarrassing to put on these 9EEE *pointe* shoes! Every time this insecurity strikes I remember Byron who, in order to lose weight, wore several heavy overcoats while playing cricket. If he could do that, then I can certainly wear my *pointe* shoes without qualm.

Toe shoes hurt! The fact that women wear them all day is remarkable. And each night on stage they move so beautifully with no trace of discomfort. I am relieved not to be a woman.

Dance is an art; a performing art. Like all performing arts it is a communication with the audience. The quality of communication determines the success of the dancer. Performing is a conversation between dancer and public. In everyday conversation, if the speaker mumbles his words, running them together, confusion ensues—the message is lost, the listener knows he heard something but is unsure what it was. The same holds true for the communication of dancing. A dancer must present each step clearly and completely before continuing. Dancing should be complete, with periods, commas, and exclamation points. This is not easy, and many dancers never perceive this. Rachel is a good example. She has a wonderful dancer's body, and more than adequate technique, but she never pauses, never completes a step before beginning the next. Fifty lines of the most beautiful poetry lose all their value if they are strung together in one long sentence without a beginning or ending. I don't suggest that a dancer should always be communicating messages of passion, despair, or death. The message might simply be movement itself. You tell the audience: "Look, here I am! Now watch. I am lifting my leg and showing it to you. *Voilà!*" Very often in rehearsals I talk out loud to myself in a similar fashion. It is a highly effective way to practice. The only case in which clarity of communication is not mandatory would be if the choreographer specified otherwise. It is the choreographer's job to make sure the message shown is beautiful. The dancer's job is to deliver it clearly.

OCTOBER

The final movement of Symphony in Three Movements. *Chore-ography by Balanchine. Music by Stravinsky.*

Roaches have a natural ability to immunize themselves to poisons. After a length of time some insecticides become useless because the roaches have grown immune to them. One must find something stronger with which to battle them . . .

I have recently grown completely immune to the light of my special wake system. It does not affect me anymore.

So just as with roaches, I had to find a more powerful method to do the job. (Christ, I can't believe that I'm comparing myself to roaches!)

Now at 8:30 the lights still come on, but they are accompanied by the stereo at full blast and the coffee pot perking. *Hallelujah*—I'm awake!

There is a crisp, biting feeling of excitement when one begins something new; like the beginning of the school year when you rush off to school with an armful of new scholastic supplies. The sharpened pencils, the new fountain pen, the clean notebook, all these things make you feel confident and excited to begin.

With equal fervor I spent $150 on new dance clothes—some colorful leotards, new sweat pants, and a pair of bright red-and-blue-striped leg warmers.

I feel as if I am beginning a crusade. King Arthur has proclaimed a quest and the knights ride off eagerly, not really knowing where they are going, but happy to have a quest.

I am going to throw myself into dancing and like the knights riding off into the woods, I don't quite know where I'm going or how to get there, but I am going nonetheless.

Men are most happy when acting impetuously and spontaneously. There is no thought involved, no practical sense—just energy pointed in a direction. I differ from these knights in only one respect: The knight's crusade is never directed at the crusader. The man is not out for himself but for others. He is after other things—off to kill, to save a town, or to catch the bad guy. How many kings have proclaimed a quest for self-improvement? How many posses have been formed by anxious men seeking to make themselves better people?

I have created my own crusade, a crusade for self-deliverance. Still, being a man, I am happy to surrender myself to a cause, and delighted not to think.

I have big teeth and an uncontrollable smile. I often have trouble speaking seriously without grinning. I may be absolutely frank, but my visage contradicts my sincerity. The only time this smile disappears is when I am concentrating intensely. It is extreme and severe. It wears like a frown on my face. Again my face contradicts my feelings, for I look miserable and brooding when I am merely concentrating and wonderfully separate from everyone. There is a part of me that is watching to see what becomes of all this work. Oh yes, work. I have worked terribly hard with a powerful intensity that is new to me and stays with me all day. From morning class to the curtain calls, I think only about dance—analyzing, working. I don't talk to anybody. I don't want to. They are only in my way right now. They distract me. I must be left to myself now. It is difficult to write anything. The energy is incredible—like an electric charge throughout my body. I hope it will continue. I pray it will not deflate.

Several days have passed and my energy level hasn't dropped for a second. I do drink lots of caffeine, however, through coffee and Coke. I'm high-strung and hypercharged. Each morning I run to the theater anxious to start the day. I look forward most to the night when the performance is over and everyone goes home. I don't go home. I change from my costume into practice clothes and run up to the main hall, which is completely dark. I must flick the fuse box to illuminate the studio. I turn on only a few lights to give the room a hazy, shadowy atmosphere, then I begin my work. It brings me a certain satisfaction to know that everyone else has gone home while I am just beginning the hardest workout of the day. I work on "Spring," the variation, that's all. I strip off all the leg warmers. Everything must be uncovered. Sometimes I even strip down to only a dance belt and shoes.

I feel just like Rocky when he trained for his big fight. I run through the variation several times in a row. Then, exhausted, I fall straight to the floor and do twenty-five sit-ups as fast as I can. Quick! Up on my feet again. I mustn't stop, mustn't rest. I go through the variation again and again, until my legs can no longer hold me. Down to the floor and twenty-five push-ups. I get up to dash through the variation again. On and on until I fall to the floor unable to move anymore. When I reach this pitifully beaten state, I drag myself up and like a drunk, stagger to the back of the studio, and try the variation one last time. I can hardly stand up now, so I go through it hunched over heaving for breath with my feet shuffling across the floor. Finally I rest. It hurts. My stomach knots terribly and my legs tighten. I let out only loud pitiful gasps of pain and exhaustion. All of this hurts me, but I get some kind of perverse pleasure from it.

Sometimes the night watchman comes into the studio. He knows I should not be there. The theater is closed. I think he finds it all so bewildering that he leaves without a word. He probably thinks I'm crazy. I'm not. I'm just determined to dance well. When that performance of "Spring" comes along, I'll only have to do the variation once, just once! Imagine how easy it will be.

I arrived very early again this morning at the coffee shop. I had not slept much. This small restaurant, run by Greeks, has served me breakfast for the last few weeks. I come in every morning and sit at the table by the window. I don't even order my food anymore. I just sit down and the waiter yells to the cook, "Scramble two wis bacon!" I know all the waiters by name: Pete, Jimmy, and Mike. Their real Greek names I cannot pronounce. They all call me "Christo." Sometimes if I don't have money, I ask Pete if I can pay tomorrow. He always says, "No problem," and smiles.

My window seat looks out on Sixty-ninth and Broadway, which, at eight o'clock, is a very busy street. A nonstop parade of men and women troop before my eyes. I sit there and try to guess where each person is going. Most mornings I would love to sit there all day, and watch the people hurrying off! I wish I could be constantly hungry so that I might eat all day and each bite would be like the first; each cup of coffee would taste as delicious as the first sip of the morning.

It's difficult to leave my window seat, especially when it's raining outside. Fortunately, it's just a few blocks to the theater. Then I soak in the large Jacuzzi. This morning I was in the Jacuzzi by nine-thirty. Class wasn't until eleven. The theater was empty. Even the girls' dressing room was dark. After shriveling in the noisy whirlpool bubbles for twenty minutes, I was startled by a noise. If I had dog's ears they would have straightened up to listen. Being human, I simply froze and listened intensely for another sound. *Bang,* a chair was knocked over; I knew that sound. There was no mistaking it. Someone was in the dressing room! It was Tuesday and the janitor cleans only on Monday, Wednesday, and Friday. Who was it? A light shone through the crack under the bathroom door. Whoever it was had turned on a light, but the light was very dim, so the main light switch was not on. This was some lesser light. I sat quietly racking my brain as to who it might be. It was too early to be another dancer. I couldn't think of anything except the violinist who was murdered at the Met, next door. She was allegedly killed by someone who worked at the theater. The more I thought about it the more I became sure I was in danger. Whoever it was knew I was in here because of the loud Jacuzzi.

Slowly I slipped out of the tub and grabbed my towel. My heart was beating so fast and loud that my whole chest seemed to convulse with each beat. I left the Jacuzzi running, feeling confident that whoever was out there had no idea I had gotten out of the tub, but I was still stuck in the bathroom. There was only one door, and it led straight into the dressing room—straight to the killer!

I heard another noise! I had to think quickly. I thought of *Marathon Man*, a thriller by William Goldman. There was a scene very similar to this. What had the boy called Babe done? I tried to remember, I had read the book several times and practically knew it by heart, but now when I needed it, memory would not serve. I walked cautiously to the door listening intently . . . He attacked! I remembered! Babe had gambled on the old proverb that offense is the best defense. He had flung the door open and dashed for his gun which was in his desk drawer. That's what I would do. I would attack! I felt a little better—but I didn't have a gun. The best I could do would be to throw my makeup at him. That was no good, and what if *he* had a gun? What could I do? Besides, Babe never made it to his gun. In fact, he hardly got out the door before being felled. No, I must do better than that.

I looked around the bathroom for a weapon. There was nothing, absolutely nothing but little pieces of Ivory soap! All I had was my towel which I wrapped into a tight ball as I quietly placed my hand on the door handle. I figured I could throw the towel into the man's face, hopefully distracting him a half second while I grabbed for his gun. I prepared myself; I took three deep breaths—one, two, three! Flinging the door open I leaped into the partially lit dressing room, the towel cocked in my arm and a sneer on my face. There was someone right in front of me! Before I had time to stop myself I hurled the towel at him and knocked him backward.

Luke was halfway into his tights, balancing on one foot. The blow from the towel sent him hopping backward and finally crashing to the floor. He lay there, feet in the air, stunned, while I stood with every muscle taut, ready to fight to the death. We didn't move for a few seconds. "What the hell are you doing here so early!" I yelled at him. He really looked confused and scared. "I'm sorry," he said. "I thought I'd come early and warm up a little before class. I'm sorry. I was just going to put on my tights and . . ." I started laughing. He looked so funny lying there with his feet in the air, apologizing for being early. I laughed at him, then he started laughing too. I realized what a sight I must have been rushing violently out of the bathroom, flinging my towel at him, and standing ready to fight—completely nude! We both felt so foolish that we promised not to tell anyone about it. Since then he and I meet often in the mornings. I think my great drive in dancing has rubbed off on him, because he is working much harder.

Luke was very impressed when I explained my reason for attacking him. "I would never have thought of that," he admitted. "Well," I said, "you see the value of reading!"

All my workouts are paying off. I can now go through the variation nine consecutive times with seventy-five sit-ups and push-ups in between. Things are moving so fast. I am moving fast, never stopping, and am very impatient. No one talks to me anymore because half the time I don't hear them anyway. I feel as though I cannot see more than three feet in front of me. Nothing else exists. My whole world revolves around me and the few feet around me. I'm getting a little like a wild man. I don't sleep more than a few hours a night, and I awaken with clenched teeth and headaches. I get angry and impatient for the day to begin. I have never felt like this before. It's a little scary. I have lost all ability to laugh. Things just don't seem humorous as they did before. I have no patience, I cannot write . . .

I did not perform tonight. During the intermissions I went on stage and ran through the variation. Now I am home early and am a little relaxed so I can analyze the morning's fantastic occurrences.

I was up at six, walking the streets. It was cold. Halloween is coming soon and all the store windows had plastic monster masks staring outward. They looked so cheap. My family never wore those dime-store outfits because we always made our own. I'll never forget my brother, covered with yellow slime, when at nine, he trick-or-treated with a cut-out pumpkin for a head. He was the pumpkin man from the *Oz* books.

I was in the studio long before class, but by the time class began I had already done my own. I always stand at one of the portable ballet barres which I place out in the middle of the studio. No one else shares it with me, for the classes are only half full. If there were someone at my barre and they distracted me, I would be annoyed. *Nothing* must distract me, *nothing* must pull me from this world. I hear voices around me, but they are all blurred, like voices in an indoor swimming pool—hollow, echoing, unintelligible.

It is impossible to be left alone. Impossible! The pianist plays a wrong note and I snap, as though I've been slapped out of a dream. I feel I could kill him for that wrong note! I want to concentrate, but Rachael makes a joke and everyone laughs. Again I am distracted. I hate her for it, I want to yell, "Don't you get tired of always being funny?" I try to get back into my own world, but it is impossible because my father is staring at me. I feel his eyes. Damn it, won't he ever leave me alone! I concentrate fiercely and block him out.

When the barre was over and we were in the center of the room watching John Taras give the next combination, I felt my father's hands on my shoulders. I stiffened: Damn him! I wanted to hit him! He lightly massaged my shoulders which were like rocks. I couldn't look at him. He said something, I don't remember what, something simple, his voice was strange, not his usual self-assured tone. It was weak, filled with love and reassurance, but confused. It seemed so pitiful. I sighed, feeling like a great weight had been lifted. I wanted to turn and hug him, but tears welled up in my eyes, and I left the studio hiding my face.

The minute I got out, I ran down the six flights of stairs to the cellar. I was crying loudly; I never cry. The cellar is a huge, damp, dusty storage room for all the scenery of the ballet and the opera. It's a whole city of different sets, different styles. I sat on a wooden crate and cried. There were so many tears, yet at the same time part of me was examining and laughing at me. This part said, "Chris, what are you doing?" For a few minutes I continued this mewling, then as though something startled me, I stopped, quickly wiped off my face, and ran back up the stairs and into class as fast as I could. I finished the class in the same intense world in which I had started it.

I think this must be what it's like to go crazy. I no longer control my actions. However, all the time a part of me is aware of the absurdity of what I am putting myself through. I let it happen. I encourage it. I'm not sure I could stop it; I think I sort of like it.

Other dancers have been making a point of talking to me these past few days. They approach me to tell me that I am looking pale and thin. They fear I may be getting sick.

"Are you eating enough?" they ask. "Are you taking vitamins?"

How silly they are. I feel physically better than I ever have in my life, and certainly stronger than ever. I don't suppose it's as obvious to others as it is to me, but I am dancing better. I feel there is a great improvement in some areas. Mostly there is a feeling of control in my dancing that I have never felt before. I am stronger with each week's end, with each nightfall.

In high school each September was the optimistic beginning of a new year. The only significance January 1 had was that most people slept through it with hangovers. In the ballet the beginning of each performing season seems like the year's commencement. I feel as if I have aged several times what the annual birthday indicates.

When I was in school, the day of the week was of vital importance. If it was Monday, better known as "Blue Monday," that meant the beginning of a long week. When Friday finally arrived the weekend came with it, and we said, "Thank God it's Friday." But now all the days are the same to me. There is no difference between Monday and Friday. I am only conscious of the days of the week by which section of the New York *Times* I read. If it's the "Living Section," then it must be Wednesday. The "Home Section"? It must be Thursday. And if the paper weighs a ton, then it's Sunday.

NOVEMBER

In the third movement of **Brahms-Schoenberg Quartet** *with Heather Watts.*

The performance of "Spring" lies three days away; in that time all the weeks of labor shall be put to the test. I have slept only ten hours throughout the past three days. I sit up late into the morning thinking intensely about nothing. I act like a man wild with a fanatical idea, yet there is nothing in my head—no thought, no ideas.

This morning I awoke with a scream. My thigh had gone into a spasm and was knotted painfully. I was gripping and kneading my thigh even before I was fully awake. I stopped for a second, removing my hands from the cramp. I looked at the twisted, rock-hard muscle. It was pushed outward in a position unnatural to the thigh. I was astonished at the immense contortion and the pain. I sat staring, not moving my hands to relieve it even though my face was screwed up from the pain. Soon I had seen enough and could no longer bear the hurt. After five minutes of wrestling with it, it calmed.

I am deeply alone, ensconced in solitude. Solitude and loneliness. For the first time I understand why people claim us to be singularly and inevitably alone. I don't like to believe that. We wish for something secure that might always be there for us. But there is nothing, only our aloneness, and it will never part from us. It is a medicine we are required to swallow. Perhaps we could learn to make it work for us. Couldn't I make solitude a friend? If I could grow comfortable with solitude, then it would become an ally, something to depend on, something secure. One can be certain of its perpetual loyalty. If I could learn to be content with solitude, then I would have gained a friend for life.

There are times when I revel in solitude and relish it. These times it is my companion. But there are other times, miserable times, when it is loneliness, not solitude, and those times I would run to a bum in the street and find anything he said interesting.

I was jinxed right off the bat. I was extremely nervous as I walked onto the stage to begin the variation. My breathing came in short sharp breaths. I took my pose with my face lifted to the audience, but my eyes affixed to the conductor's baton. I watched his hand move but there seemed to be no audible emanation of music from the pit. I stiffened with panic and listened. There was music, but I couldn't recognize any rhythm. I was forced to begin in confusion. Tentatively, I stepped into the first leap. As my feet left the floor the music finally became recognizable—I was late!

What followed was disastrous. My feet cramped like knotted clubs that would neither point nor hold me on balance. I was immediately drained of breath following the opening two steps. I was horrified. What about all my workouts? What happened? I was like Superman dancing on a stage of Kryptonite. I had no strength, no stamina. It must have looked pitiful, my flopping around. Jesus, I could have danced that badly without the painful weeks of preparation!

Following the completion of the ballet, I stepped briskly to the dressing room, avoiding anyone's direct glance. It was embarrassing. Jerry was out of town, and I was thankful for that. I sulked in the dressing room feeling as beaten as a defeated soldier returning home to face the family in disgrace. My parents slipped in to see me. They both agreed that I had done well. They had expected less of me and were surprisingly complimentary. Their praise embarrassed me. They believed what they said, but they didn't realize how much better I had planned on dancing. Well, what did I expect. A transformation into Mr. Colossal in a few weeks? I suppose it takes more time. Oh, but it all seemed so worthless, so futile. What was the point? What did I work myself so frantically for? So that I would be miserably disappointed with the outcome? Hell, I could have gone out drinking with Luke, had a wonderful time, and still have been equally unhappy with my performance. I really wonder about the point of all this; why bother? I doubt if I'll ever be comfortable on the stage. Will I ever acquire the ability to dance with the quality of which my mind is aware?

In the "Spring" section of The Four Seasons *with Judith Fugate.*

A blessing of this profession is that last night's performance is readily forgotten this morning, and there is an upcoming one to worry about today. Back in the theater everything has returned to its previous arrangement. "Spring" will not be performed again this season. Thank goodness for that! I don't think I could take it again. This turbulent performance has left me scarred, yet no one else here seems to even remember that I danced last night. All is forgotten, and everything is right back to normal. However, there is one exciting addition.

Mr. B. has recovered brilliantly from his heart operation, and is frequenting the theater daily. I am glad to see him, although we hardly share words. Not many of the dancers ever speak to him, particularly the younger ones. He is a living legend, and his long absence has made him like a God to us. He walks into a room and everyone notices, but only a few acknowledge him. How can we speak to a God on our own level? We cannot say, "Hey, God, how ya doing? Listen, there's this great pizza parlor right around the corner . . ." No, I don't dare approach him unless I feel I have something to say that is worthy of his ears. My father laughs at this deification. He says if I do approach Mr. B. with some great profound statement, he would probably look at me and say, "Yes that is true, but did you know there's a great pizza parlor right around the corner?"

Now I sleep. Fourteen hours, in fact. I have called Rosemary to let her know that I am sick. Simply worn down I suppose, and disillusioned.

> "If I were a medical man, I should prescribe a holiday
> to any patient who considered his work important."
> BERTRAND RUSSELL

I read this now, but it's a little late. Besides, books can influence my future actions, enlighten my past, but they can never dissuade me from obsession. To think of it now, I see my past weeks' actions as absurd. I believe I have touched upon the land of insanity. Just a little peek. Now I know that the path is open to me.

I am reminded of our recent Copenhagen tour. I had opened the window of my hotel room to see if the weather had improved. The view overlooked the courtyard of the Town Hall. After pulling open the windows and leaning out upon the ledge I was taken aback by the scene outside. As usual, the rain was heavy and the sky dark, but in the courtyard was a spectacle of extraordinary peculiarity. Wrapped in brightly colored raincoats were perhaps fifty men and women. They all faced each other, linking hands to form a large circle. They chanted some unintelligible song and *danced!*

After pondering this scene for some moments, I was convinced that I failed to perceive the subtle explanation of this absurd spectacle. Certainly there must have been a logical reason for this folklike dancing in the pouring rain. I recorded them quickly with my Instamatic, then descended into the lobby to get some further information.

"They're crazy," said the porter.

"Yes," I laughed, "I suppose they are."

"No, I mean they *are* really crazy!" he persisted.

"What do you mean crazy?"

He explained that they were mentally weak people who had all suffered breakdowns. They were protesting in front of the Town Hall, demanding recognized rights. Lunatic rights! Their argument was that every man and woman is subjected to tremendous stress and anxiety daily. Most people harness these pressures, stifling them, and forcing an unnatural mental dictation upon the natural body functions. To act totally naturally—to allow nature's course to proceed unimpeded—one should vent these pressures. So they all had experienced nervous breakdowns. They were claiming that we, the majority, were actually the abnormal ones, and that they should be recognized as normal.

Perhaps they were right; insanity wasn't so bad. I even enjoyed it. Maybe the real route to happiness lies in insanity.

Elenore, a dear friend of my parents, was told by doctors at the age of twelve that she must give up ballet dancing because of a heart problem. Subsequently, she discovered the doctors' diagnosis to have been ridiculous, but it was too late for her to return to dance. In the interim she became, among other things, a practicing psychiatrist. She told me that most of the deeply insane patients are miserable and horribly depressed. "But one man," she said, "used to walk into the office on cloud nine. He was always bursting with joy. To society he was a wreck with absolutely no sense of responsibility, but it didn't bother him. Nothing bothered him. I didn't know whether I should try to help him or to learn from him."

Demonstrators in Copenhagen.

Last night on the rehearsal tapes it was announced that there would be an hour union meeting this morning to discuss the per diem for next summer's tour. Per diem, or "per day," is the money we are paid over our normal salaries to cover expenses while on tour. We are scheduled to dance ten days in Copenhagen, one week in Berlin, and two weeks in Paris.

I arrived five minutes late to this meeting. The small room was crowded with dancers sitting in chairs or on the floor and standing around the sides. The number of dancers present was not large, but neither was the number of square feet to the room, hence the crowding.

Seated at a table was a large, formally dressed man of austere countenance. He was our union representative and was addressing the dancers as I entered. It appeared that plans for Copenhagen and Berlin were settled to everyone's satisfaction, but Paris was a problem. The discrepancy was over how much per diem we would be receiving there. The cost of the Paris hotels would be so colossal that we would have little per diem left to eat on.

One of the dancers was being very authoritative about it all. "We must stick together on this," she crusaded. "Tell them if we don't get more money, then we are not going." At this time I felt an ulcerous twist in my stomach and left the room. As I left, I felt like asking her, "Do you want to dance or go shopping?" My chicken heart made me slip out quietly, but I was shocked. Even if the per diem *only* covered the hotel rooms, we would still receive our normal pay checks so no one would lose money. If we are smart, we sublet our apartments and come out way ahead. What's the problem?

I wonder what the reaction would be if they announced the tour by saying: "Look, we can't pay you much, but we'll take you to Europe for five weeks to dance. Would you like to go?" How could anyone refuse?

Security and surplus are often followed by luxury; a television set for example. The television, which is a luxury to the proud couple who used to be radio enthusiasts, is taken for granted by their children. When the TV breaks down the parents find entertainment in the old radio, but the children are unsatisfied. They will demand leave of the house to watch the neighbor's TV rather than hear the radio which, by the way, was the luxury of their grandparents. This is a natural course. It must be avoided in the arts. The generation of artists that has matured accustomed to plush conditions must not balk at lesser standards.

We call people who grow up with luxury "spoiled." There is no fault in being spoiled as long as the person is aware of this weal and will be undaunted to settle for less. In NYCB we are all spoiled. Certainly we should have all attainable advancements in standards, but the point is that all artists, at any level, should harbor within their artistic values a humility amid prosperity.

Most reputations are based on some relative fact. Every stereotype has some quality to justify the title.

"Actors are neurotic."

"Dancers are boring."

"Beautiful blondes are dumb."

All of these clichés can bear explanation. Many of the actors I have met are not contented people. An actor is always analyzing himself because his job depends on his ability to analyze characters. But excessive self-analyzation can drive one crazy! Someone may discover more intricacies of personality than he is able to reconcile. This indulgence in analysis is prevalent in the profession of acting, and that might explain the origin of its reputation.

But what about the beautiful dumb blonde?

This title does not pertain solely to people in a specialized profession. Physical appearance is what labels them. So where is the truth in the stereotype? It is not the blond hair that makes one dumb; it is the person's beauty that really contributes. For example:

Young Jessica joined the company only a year before me. I knew her when she was in the school. She has a cute kind of beauty that attracts everyone.

Caroline, her best friend, was not so pretty. She was not unattractive, but not often noticed. Caroline had a rounded, homely country girl appearance; Jessica had the look of a sleek city girl.

Ever since I first saw Jessica I have had a crush on her, and so does everybody else. In all the years I have known her, I have never seen her alone. None of her friendships were anything more than "friendships of necessity."

Caroline broke away from Jessica for to be in Jessica's company left her practically unnoticed. Any boys who stumbled upon them saw only Jessica. Caroline had to discover another method to attract the boys. She sought to widen her interests, and she developed other qualities of her personality, which had not been previously evident. She read extensively, she conversed with everybody, and learned about them and from them.

All the while Jessica went on being entertained.

As fate would have it, first Jessica, then later Caroline, joined the company. Now I work with them every day, and have discovered, quite unexpectedly, that I greatly prefer Caroline to Jessica. Although Jessica still has the physical attractiveness that will always excite me, Caroline has grown beautiful. Her features are the same, but it is her personality, her development of mind that has transformed her.

The point of all this is that had Caroline also been the attractive success that Jessica was, she would have never sought anything more. *Because* she was not beautiful she developed her mind, which, in turn, made her beautiful.

This is a common occurrence, but it can never happen the other way. A terrific mind can render an ugly woman beautiful, but beauty can never transform a lack of intelligence.

My friends, upon reading this last page, have cautioned me that I might offend all the beautiful women with these statements. I would venture a guess that the type I describe would never be reading this book. So, if you, reader, are beautiful, consider yourself an exception.

What is true for the beautiful woman is also true for the dancer. Quite often the dancer with tremendous talent, the one to whom everything comes quite easily, does nothing more than simply exhibit his ability, while the ones to whom things come with difficulty must make the most of what they have, and often they become better dancers than the naturally gifted.

Bart Cook is an example. I feel great reverence toward him. He is a principal dancer in the company. He is not an exquisitely handsome man. He is not an impressive figure. He does not have an extreme elevation, nor can he perform multiple *pirouettes*. These are the common prerequisites for the major male dancer. He has strength in none of these. However, put him on the stage and I won't watch anyone else—this statement does not include women, so I had better rephrase it. Put him on the stage and I won't watch any other man. He is the admirable example of someone making much out of little. Every step he does, every arm movement or twist of the head is carefully analyzed and rehearsed so he can make the most of it. And with that practice he combines spontaneity so that his performances never look mechanical. He is not a classical ballet dancer. He would not excel in the difficult classical roles. He is most interesting in the more unique and specialized ballets.

Bart is an artist. That is the best compliment. Although dance is an art, I would not call all dancers artists. Bart is not a technician, not a flashy entertainer. He takes what is given him—the choreography, the music, and his body—and works with them all to make something special, something great.

I was very lazy today. It was one of those days when lack of energy and inspiration easily overthrow the desire for a strong sense of discipline.

The most tedious stretch of the day would be a two-hour rehearsal of *Chaconne* on stage. *Chaconne* is a Balanchine ballet to the music of Gluck. It is a gloriously elegant vehicle for Suzanne Farrell.

Unfortunately, the corps part is minimal. I have been dancing in *Chaconne* since June, so the prospect of a two-hour rehearsal was tedious. Reluctantly, I shuffled down to the stage, anticipating a major "marking" of the rehearsal.

When I reached the stage I realized that marking was out of the question. For there, dressed in a dark green jacket with a red scarf around his neck, was Balanchine. He was standing by the piano watching the dancers wander in. I began warming up immediately.

The stage was void of scenery as is usual in the afternoon. The curtain was raised, revealing 2,700 empty seats. The rehearsal began five minutes late.

Mr. B. stood at the front of the stage, his heels almost touching the footlights. He has a grand posture, one for which he is well renowned. It enables him to appear to be looking down at you although he is not tall. He watched in silence as Suzanne and Peter Martins danced the first *pas de deux*. Neither Sue nor Peter spoke as they rehearsed. When they finished, we danced our short opening section. We received no response from Mr. B.

Our section is followed by a series of short dances one of which involves five small girls. It was these girls Mr. B. stopped. Midway through their dance he halted the music. He looked at one of the girls.

"You know, dear," he began, "you dance like you are asleep. If you are asleep, audience is asleep too."

The girl said nothing. She just shrugged her shoulders.

Mr. B. continued. "I want to see energy, all the energy you have. Otherwise no one will pay twenty dollars to see you. Now again."

All five girls lined up for the beginning of the dance. They had hardly repeated the first step when he stopped them again.

"No. No."

He walked toward the same girl. "Just do the first step," he demanded, stopping just in front of her. She did it.

"Bigger," he persisted.

She repeated the step a little bigger. Mr. B. was not satisfied. "Dear, do it one last time, and when you finish you will die. That will be the end of your life. Now I want to see."

He stepped back a few feet and waited. Again she repeated the step.

Apparently it wasn't good enough, for Mr. B. threw up his hands, turned and walked back to the footlights.

"You know," his final remarks were, "better to die now a hero than to live a coward for a hundred years!"

He was silent for the rest of the rehearsal. At the end of the second hour I was exhausted. For although the finale is brief, I discharged all the energy I could muster, just in case he stopped watching Suzanne and glanced my way.

I had just finished Jerome Robbins' *Opus 19—The Dreamer*. I changed out of my sweaty blue costume and into the clean, dry, yellow leotard for another Robbins ballet, *Fanfare*. Balanchine's *Kammermusik* was just beginning. It was to be followed by an intermission and then *Fanfare*.

I was well warmed up after the first ballet and my makeup was still intact, so I threw on my bright green sweat pants and jumped my way down the stairs to the stage to watch *Kammermusik*. I still had not learned it all.

Rehearsal with Mr. B.

The wings were so crowded that I could not find a clear view of the stage. I decided to do some *pliés* and *tendus* at the barre.

As I turned from the wing a large figure of a man with dark curly hair caught my eye. He was standing beside the prop table trying to watch the performance from there. I recognized him immediately. It was Kurt Vonnegut. To my joy he also recognized me. I had met him once before and had showered him with the enthusiasm I felt for his books. We shook hands and exchanged "How do you dos." He explained that he was meeting one of the dancers after the performance and was going out to dinner. I worried that he might not be able to see the stage very well from where he stood, but he assured me that he was content, so I left him to watch and returned to the barre for my *pliés*.

I was so excited that I whispered to every dancer who passed near me, "Do you know Kurt Vonnegut?" Most of them replied affirmatively.

"Well, he's standing right over there." I would nonchalantly incline my head in his direction.

"Is it really?" they would ask. "Are you sure?"

"Of course," I'd exclaim indignantly. I was thrilled.

But pretty soon my game ended for no one else passed by to share my secret with. So I took to looking at him out of the corner of my eye as I merely went through the motions of a serious warm-up. He was standing quietly in the darkness. His face, however, was illuminated by the stage lights. He seemed fascinated with the performance. His eyes gleamed with excitement and love.

I got the feeling as I watched him that if he had the choice, he would start all over again as a performer. I believe he loves writing—it shows in his books—but watching the dancers on stage seemed to boil his blood.

I suddenly felt proud to be where I was. I wonder how many people are frustrated performers. New York is full of them: punk rockers, disco dancers, Frisbee players, roller skaters . . . everyone performs wherever they can.

When I looked over again, he was gone. Off to dinner. Who knows where. Off to write again, I hoped. I continued my work now feeling extra inspiration.

Occasionally the timing of fate is ideal. Not often. Sometimes things occur exactly when one is best prepared for them. More often fate will dictate the most untimely occurrence.

There was something about Jerome Robbins' *Fancy Free* that attracted me instantly. Maybe it was the story line, or perhaps because it was danced in sailor suits and character shoes. Character shoes look like street shoes and don't allow one's feet to point much, so a bad arch goes unnoticed. I took to the ballet immediately. In the same dissecting manner in which Bart works on a new role, I practiced *Fancy Free,* more than was called for, especially since I was only the understudy. I was an extremely well-prepared understudy.

The first cast of the ballet was also well rehearsed and ready to go for the NYCB premiere, which was in two weeks. To our surprise, another rehearsal was called for Bart, Jean-Pierre Frolich, myself, and the other understudies. It was peculiar that I was the understudy yet was not listed as such for this rehearsal. Was Peter Martins injured? Or perhaps he just couldn't come to the rehearsal and Jerry needed the understudy to fill in. That must have been the explanation. It didn't matter, I was well prepared. I knew it inside out.

I pulled out my old faded denim jeans. They fit just like the sailor pants might. I had been using them for rehearsals. I wore my well-broken-in black character shoes and a plain white shirt. These looked just like street clothes, not rehearsal attire, but this was not an ordinary ballet.

Jerry came into the rehearsal looking a little harassed. I felt almost thankful that I wasn't the first cast because he wouldn't spend much time on me.

He gave us the four-clap introduction and I made the first entrance. "STOP," Jerry yelled. "You're already late, Chris," he scolded. I started again.

"STOP," he repeated. "You have to travel more, otherwise the audience cannot see you."

I was getting panicky. Something was peculiar here. He was acting as if I were going to be doing this on opening night. I got more excited and agitated, and already my T shirt was soaked with sweat.

As the rehearsal progressed I became more and more certain that I was being prepared for the first performance. He practically ignored the other two sailors. I was getting a complete workover.

Finally, at the end of the two hours it was time for the variations. I had the third and final one. Jerry completely skipped the other two—he wanted to see if I knew mine. This time he didn't stop me. He just let me run through it. I was very happy and dancing very well. Near the end of the variation came the biggest jumps of the dance. I do a *tour jeté* and a twist. This is not really a difficult jump. It involved kicking both legs into the air and twisting, landing on one leg and immediately going into another jump.

Since my technical attributes are weak, I must always exploit that which I do best. I may not have the perfect body for ballet, but I can jump! Thank God I can jump! That was something I inherited from my parents. When I jump the audience may not witness the finest classical position in the air, my arms may be sloppy and my feet not curved enough, but they'll have a hell of a long time to see it!

As I prepared for these jumps I was sure I had the role. For whatever reason, Peter was not going to do it and I was up to bat. But just to make sure, I did t' ʾ first jump higher than usual, kicking both legs and landing perfectly. Then, again the second time, I jumped higher than ever, holding the position in the air just a half a second longer than usual. From that peak I seemed to go straight to the floor. I'm still not sure how it happened. Somehow I miscalculated my landing and hit the floor on the side of my foot, twisting it and falling face down to the ground. "Terrific," I thought to myself. "That will really impress him." I got up quickly and tried to catch up with the music . . . well, that's what I had intended to do. But sudden pain overwhelmed me and again I found myself with my face on the floor! I yelled "My foot!" It hurt like I couldn't believe. There was a throbbing pain, and I punched my fist hard on the floor to somehow relieve it.

Luke was pulling off my shoe. He had been watching from the doorway and rushed in when I fell. He is the type who acts instantly while others are stunned—Luke would be the one to yank you from the path of an onrushing automobile. He gasped upon removing the sock. I straightened up and looked. There on the side of my arch was a lump the size of a golf ball! "Oh my God!" I couldn't believe that my foot could do that. If it swelled any more I was afraid it might burst. Luke leaned over and picked me up. "Come on, you have to get it under ice."

Things began to blur a little. Someone went for ice while Luke carried me to the bathroom and stuck my foot under the cold running faucet. Oh, it hurt! It really hurt. Jerry came in with a wet towel and wiped my sweaty forehead. I whispered, "I'm sorry, Jerry."

Ice packs and Ace bandages arrived and were wrapped around the foot. Luke handed me a pair of crutches.

"There's a car downstairs to take you to the hospital."

"What's the point?" I sighed. "I'm going to miss *Fancy Free.*"

I went nonetheless.

The doctor's office was filled with patients, but luckily I was taken in immediately and hoisted onto the X-ray table.

"It's not broken," the doctor said in his southern voice, "but it's a very serious sprain."

I was relieved that it wasn't broken. "How long will it take?" I prayed he would say only one week.

"Well, it's hard to say with a sprain. If it were broken it would probably take four weeks." It wasn't broken, so I hoped for a maximum two weeks off.

"But a sprain like this usually takes anywhere from four to six weeks."

"What? I can't be out that long!" I yelled at him.

"Well, I'm sorry, but that's the way it looks. Now go home and keep ice on it."

I went to my parents' house. Since I could not move around for a few days, I couldn't be alone in my apartment. I lay on the living room sofa bed, because my old room was three flights up which was too much for me and my crutches. My foot was still aching, and I was dying for a drink.

It all still seemed so unbelievable. I just would not acknowledge that I would be unable to dance in the morning, or the day after. I consoled myself by saying aloud, "This won't stop me. I'll take a few days off and come back again." My mind heartily encouraged these thoughts, but my body disagreed. This was the first time I realized that my body was not invincible as I had believed it to be. Still, I persisted in entertaining the notion of a quick recovery. I put on several heavy ice bags and left them tightly wrapped around my swollen foot. It was torture for the first fifteen minutes, then the whole foot gradually numbed. I figured that twice the prescribed length of icing would ensure twice the speed of healing.

After two hours of ice I hastily removed the wrappings to examine the foot. I was not pleasantly surprised.

Not only had the golf ball remained, but the whole side of my foot was blue! I had frozen it! My mind immediately leaped to thoughts of gangrene and the amputation of my foot. Jesus! That did it. I finally realized that I was to be out for some time.

DECEMBER

Robbins' Piano Pieces.

How awful to be injured! It's like waking from a horrible nightmare and sitting up all night waiting for morning. Everything is well in the morning, yet in this long nightmare the arrival of morning is undetermined. "FOUR TO SIX WEEKS!"

Now, after a week, I am allowed to move around. The first few days after the fall I sat propped up in bed with ice around my foot. Fortunately, I had not frozen the foot, or, if I had, it thawed.

A day without movement was a frustration to which I was unaccustomed. If my sisters hadn't been there entertaining me, I would have been totally miserable. I did get to move a little: I breathed, I moved my right arm from plate to mouth, and used the same arm to manipulate the television. But I itched to move; oh, the ecstasy that simple walking would have brought! Presently the crutches accompany me in this action.

I pass most of the day sleeping and watching TV, with absolutely zero energy. I want to sleep as much as possible; when I awaken I lie in bed for hours wondering, "Why should I get up?" Thank God for food, it is my only rapture. In the past I have complained about the many desires that dancing keeps me from pursuing. Now I have all the time I could need and I slouch around like the apathetic Oblomov, Ivan Goncharov's leading character, who led a life of exclusive sleeping and eating.

I have heard that Russians who have defected to the U.S.A. are at a loss as to how to use their newly acquired freedom. They are accustomed to being told what to do, and they have little experience at making decisions. It is the same with me. I have grown used to calling the rehearsal tape each night and being told what my day would hold. I still call the tape anyway, just to hear what I am missing. *Fancy Free* will premiere without me. Peter will do it after all. In between meals I watch all the afternoon soaps, and when there is nothing left to watch on the tube I resort to daydreaming about how I had planned on dancing *Fancy Free*. Reminiscing is a common pastime of old people. I feel like an old man who is no longer able to participate in life. I just sit around and remember how I lived.

I have judged the events of the past months, particularly my extreme preparation for "Spring." I really enjoyed that masochistic time, but now it seems clearly excessive. I went too far. The way to improvement lies in the consistency of the effort, not in the amount of work. Rather than working oneself to death with fifteen hours a day of extreme labor for three weeks, it is better to work five hours a day for months. This method allows the body to grow into the change rather than leap forward with you hoping your body will sustain you.

I went back to the theater, I suppose simply to torture myself. Or maybe just to get attention. I certainly was dramatic, crutching around backstage. Some dancers came up to me to find out what had happened. They hadn't known I was out! Other people just walked by as if they didn't see me. A few people in passing asked, "How's your knee?" My knee? For Christ's sake, didn't they see the bandages around my foot?

Well, all this just lends support to my disliking of "friendships of necessity."

Our lives are so involved with dancing and totally encompassed by the windowless theater that the outside world has little effect on us. There could be a thunder and lightning storm going on outside and we might never know. Once something leaves this world it is quickly forgotten. It then belongs to the vast *outside*, which has so little value from the inside. It's not really a surprise that one is so quickly forgotten. Actually, they didn't desert me, I simply could not keep up with them. I'm the deserter!

Hell, I might as well be in another country. Luke checked up on me the first day, but even he has forgotten. I don't blame him really. I would probably do the same.

I left the stage realizing that I must not return until I am able to dance again. I crutched down the hall to the main rehearsal room which was empty. I stood in the middle of the vast floor and looked in the mirror. Just a short time ago I was working there. I smiled to remember all the torturous push-ups and sit-ups. Now I was torturing myself again by entering the same room but being unable to work.

I threw down the crutches and hopped around on one foot. Perhaps I could come here every day and work just on one foot. No, that was absurd—it has to be all or nothing. I retrieved the fallen crutches and went home.

I really miss not being surrounded by all the beautiful ballerinas. I realize that I take them for granted. One should never take beautiful women for granted. On and on I rave about my adoration of women, yet at the same time I almost despise them. I hate their monumental effect on me. It is unfair for I am helpless against them. They can dissuade me from the direst of matters, with the tritest.

Women are like a disease, one that I have no natural defenses against. This disease is constantly upsetting the system, making me unable to function properly.

I hate to admit it, but it is the beauty that does it. Absolutely. Beauty is undefeatable. When I meet a beautiful energetic woman, I become an instant alchemist, doing my best to transform any of her bad qualities into good.

Jessica has always held me captive by her attractiveness. For nine months I have worked with her practically every day. I fear she is only indifferent to me. For nine months she has made me unhappy. I don't suggest that she ruins my life, merely that she is a constant frustration. A perpetual itch that I can never scratch.

The fact is that there is only a physical attraction. I know this and (here comes the horrifying part) no matter how hard I try, I cannot defeat her effect on me!

She has no idea of her power. If she were somehow doing it on purpose then I would feel a little better.

I tried to completely ignore her, I simply looked the other way when she was in sight—*no avail!*

I tried the opposite—I looked at her constantly, hoping to lose interest through overexposure—like the man who works in the bakery who cannot stand cake because of his overexposure to the smell—*no avail!*

I tried getting to know her, hoping that her lack of personality would discourage me—*no avail!*

I would try to make her fall for me, but that would be the most torturous process. Hell, I'll try anyway. I have to do something.

It's not fair! What did I do to deserve this?

Do women feel the same way about men? Almost every night when I close my eyes to sleep I think about women. That's awful.

And worse than that, I have thought about almost every girl in the company. I don't even *like* some of them! What perversion is this? I bet that most of the straight men in the company close their eyes with the same thoughts. Do women?

One night at a large dinner party I posed the question.

There was a twenty-foot table with everyone from young girls to old men around it. To gain the attention of so many people is not difficult. All one need do is speak clearly either of these two words: BLOOD or SEX.

You might say, "Oh, and there was BLOOD everywhere!"

Or perhaps, "My God, you wouldn't have believed the SEX!"

Either one of these phrases will arrest all other conversation, and for an instant all the heads will turn in your direction. I used the latter phrase, and gaining full attention, I asked the question:

"How many men go to bed thinking of women, and how many women think of men?"

Everyone was sufficiently inebriated so as to allow for free-flowing honesty.

All but one of the men admitted to the act. The women said that once in a while they thought about men, but most often they weren't sure what was on their minds.

Well, if this is true for most women, then it's just not fair.

What am I to do about Jessica? Maybe I ought to start thinking about the possibilities of rape. Well, I wouldn't go that far!

I am often ashamed how little I care about the factual side of dancing. I never read about ballet. I dance all day. I don't want to go home on a free night and read about how other people dance all day also. I never go to see the ballet. I realize that one might learn much about how to dance and choreograph by seeing every dance company around. But when it comes to going out on a free night, I'd much rather go see a movie or a show. I am absolutely ignorant about dance history. I don't care. I love the DANCING! That's it. That's all that matters. When good music plays I simply cannot help but move to it. Knowing more about the history of dance will not enhance this feeling. So for those who don't find dancing satisfying, or for those who don't dance at all, let them know the history. Let them evaluate the facts. I'll have none of it!

As we grow older, it becomes increasingly difficult to learn. Eventually it becomes a task simply to recall what has already been learned. There is less patience, and the desire to relearn anything is lost. "It's easier to teach an old dog new tricks than to unteach the old tricks." For example, I shall never throw out feet and inches for the metric system. Nor would I even want to try. Inches work fine for me; why waste time going back and relearning? However, I believe that if I took a serious look at the metric system, I would agree wholeheartedly that it is superior. But even then I would not bother to change, because "MY WAY WORKS FINE FOR ME." I believe it is this attitude that is primarily responsible for Baryshnikov's unhappiness with and finally his departure from NYCB.

At the height of success, Mischa picked up and left the American Ballet Theatre, where he was making thousands of dollars a performance. Money was certainly not his objective in joining us. Some people claimed that he sought to inherit Balanchine's shoes, but I believe it was simply artistic reasons that brought Mischa to Balanchine. He wanted to work with the greatest choreographer and dance the greatest ballets. Many of the Balanchine ballets require a physical prowess that is different from what one gets through ordinary training. Much of this was new to Mischa. He found himself dancing ballets in which big leaps and *pirouettes* were not needed, where drama and keen musicality were prevalent. You have to know how Mr. B. wants you to move to be able to get the most out of his ballets, or rather to give the most to his ballets.

As a dancer develops, he incorporates a style, a certain panache, which adorns his dancing. Once a dancer takes on his individual style it becomes visible in everything he dances. A ballet career is short-lived. Once a dancer becomes comfortable with his way of dancing, he is already halfway through his career. And as he gets older and less dexterous, his style is the only remaining thing that keeps him special.

For Mischa to truly succeed with Balanchine, he would have had to become a student again, to start from scratch and relearn everything. He would have had to relinquish the crown and become Balanchine's pupil. Mischa didn't want to. Who can blame him? To start over at thirty? At the last stretch of his dancing career? So he became uncomfortable in NYCB. This company just wasn't right for him. I regret his leaving. He was very inspiring to me. But I think he is better off now. He is a truly great dancer. But a dancer is never perfect, never reaches all his goals. For Mischa, more improvement would have meant starting over. He came here, a master on his feet. So why should he start calling them meters?

I have discovered something wonderful. It's called a wine cooler. It is made of a tall glass of ice, half a cup of red wine, and half a cup of 7-Up. I drink it like water. In fact, I drink a little too much of it. Each night I put on the stereo and sit with my feet up, downing several large glasses of coolers.

My conscience whispers: "If you start with wine at nineteen you'll be hooked on the hard stuff by twenty-five!" I ignore this irritating voice. I never worry about starting bad habits. I always know that if a habit got out of hand and impeded my functioning, then I'd quit. Just like that. In fact, I enjoy challenging myself to quit bad habits. It's like another crusade, another adventure. I actually look forward to starting a bad habit, because I know I'll enjoy indulging in it, and then I'll enjoy breaking it.

It is disconcerting that the last weeks, being devoid of dancing, have not made me miserable. I have no trouble sleeping, eating, and laughing. I hardly think about dance anymore. I don't call the tape anymore. But I have frequent nightmares about ballet. Through my eighteen years I have never dreamed about ballet. Now repeatedly I am a victim of disquieting reveries. Most of them are crisis dreams:

I am sitting comfortably in the dressing room, in makeup and costume, listening casually to the music over the intercom. Then I realize that the music playing is the cue for my entrance! Quickly, I scramble out of the room and dash for the stairs. Leaping the whole twelve steps at a time I descend frantically. In reality it is only two flights down to the stage, but in the dream I leap from floor to floor relentlessly, all the while hearing the music. I never make it. The ballet is over and I am still tumbling down the stairs . . .

Some dreams may be frightening, but they are often too wild and fantastic to be believable. The more alarming dreams are the possible ones:

With great force the heavy metal door to my father's dressing room swings open. I am sitting at his makeup table using his nail clippers.

"Chris!" my father yells, rushing into the room. "Listen, my foot is bad, I can hardly walk, you'll have to go on for me!"

"What ballet?" I demand, hoping it is something I know well. He names a ballet I have never heard of.

"But I've never even seen that ballet," I say.

"Sure you have, we've rehearsed it several times."

"Rehearsed it? I've never even heard of it!" My complaints are in vain, he pushes me toward the stage.

"Who do I have to dance with?" I am feeling suddenly queasy.

"Suzanne."

"You've got to be kidding! But I don't know the ballet! . . ."

Blinded by white lights I find myself on stage. The wings are seething a thick mist, and the curtain is raised. Nothing is visible but the excess whiteness. I, costumed in white, shiver. Standing before me, also in a bleached dress, is Suzanne. She seems impossibly tall, like a giant. I shudder, not from the common nerves of being on stage, but from a monumental terror of, skinny and knock-kneed, being faced with supporting this crystal tower! Unrecognizable music emanates from the mist, and Suzanne, without seeming aware of me, begins to move. I freeze. She unfolds one of her long legs and slowly does an *arabesque*. Then, with a slow deliberate movement of her head she turns her pale lips toward me and mumbles, "Hold me." I lurch and grab her waist. I hold her on balance for a few seconds when I hear her voice again. "Lift me." I hoist her up into the air and walk across the stage.

Slowly the tide turns. I am filled with some mystic knowledge of what Suzanne will do and what is required of me. I relax and smile. Soon I begin to excel. But something in Suzanne changes. She begins making it difficult for me, she resents me somehow. As we finish a series of lifts and I put her down gently by the mist-filled wing, she points a long skinny finger into the smoke and says, "*Go*."

I look into the mist. I don't want to go, but Sue leaves me and dances back to center stage. "The hell if I'm going into that mist," I say to myself and run back toward Sue who thinks I have left. I grab her waist and push her high above my head, running across the stage all the while. She writhes and twists to free herself. I will not put her down or stop running even though I am heading toward the orchestra pit. Then, like Pegasus, the flying horse, we take flight and soar easily over the orchestra and out above the audience. We fly out the front lobby and high into the air above the Lincoln Center Plaza. We climb higher, up above any building around. I look down to see the fountain in the center of the plaza.

Then Suzanne flies away on her own, and like a cartoon character who suddenly realizes that there is no ground beneath him, I pause momentarily and then fall.

I woke up immediately with a surprisingly vivid recollection of this dream. I don't really know the validity of analyzing dreams. I wouldn't even begin to try with this one. But dreams come from our unconscious minds, and the recurrence of these ballet dreams makes me suspicious that ballet is more deeply rooted in my nature than in my consciousness.

I managed to crutch off to a show tonight. Being burdened with free time these days I had thought about going to see Glenda Jackson in a play called *Rose*. Tonight was closing night so it was my last chance.

I rode on the bus down to Times Square. I could not bear the stalled traffic, and I hopped out (literally) at Fiftieth Street and crutched down to the forties where the theater was.

Unfortunately, the traffic was worse on the sidewalks than in the streets. Times Square always bustles with people going someplace, and with people watching the people going someplace. You get the feeling that the *voyeurs* are not looking at you, but at what you have that they might take advantage of.

"Don't look at the gang of big black men," I said to myself, "just pass by unnoticed." What a hypocrite! I'd never let myself pass by unnoticed on stage!

Here at Times Square are truly the lowest of people. And mind you, they are men, these rogues. Like vultures they await the opportunity to pick your pocket, to frighten you, to whistle at your woman while *their* women are out selling flesh for the little profit their pimps will allow.

"Loose joints," they mumbled as I passed as if they were not speaking to me at all but to the sidewalk. I felt like screaming, *"What?* I didn't hear you. Could you speak a little louder!"

"Loose joints." Ha! I laughed to myself, "no, actually my joints are a little tight tonight."

But all this is not fair. What a sordid account of the city I live in and love.

Times Square also bustles with people from out of town who are off to see the latest Broadway hit. There are many New Yorkers here, but one doesn't notice them because they are trained, as I am, to pass unnoticed . . .

As I passed several porno houses and peep shows one of the neon signs caught my eye.

25¢ PEEP SHOW.

I remembered this particular place, having spent some time, cautiously, within. Next door to it was another movie house, not showing an X-rated movie, but Walt Disney's *Alice in Wonderland,* rated G.

There is the real joke. All year exasperated parents wait for a movie for their children that isn't about crime and sex. When it finally arrives they cannot take their children to the theater without exposing them to crime and sex!

One night Luke and I were out at a jazz club. We ate and drank quite to the point of surfeit then walked up through Times Square. As we passed the sign 25¢ PEEP SHOW I said to him, "I've always wondered what those places are really like."

"Come on then," he said, and we did. We each paid a dollar at the door and received four tokens printed with little nude ladies.

There was a large room fitted with almost a hundred little booths, just like phone booths only smaller, and with no window. On the outside of each booth was a photo and a caption which informed one of the sort of peep show that could be expected from that booth. We picked one at random because they all seemed alike. In order to save tokens we squeezed into one booth together. After using up a few tokens we left quietly with our curiosity not just assuaged but slaughtered.

Now I bypassed the peep show, remembering the eerie-looking faces of the men who really patronized the place. I crutched off to the theater wondering, as I often have, how, amid such degeneracy, exists the greatest theater in America?

The foot has healed well. I will be able to plunge back into that windowless theater within a week. Back to dancing. No more "General Hospital" (my favorite afternoon soap opera). One hundred percent dance calls me again. I already feel like I'm too old, as if it is too late for me now.

151

If only I had danced one hundred percent from the start, from age seven!

But I wonder about that. A youth of only dance does not guarantee the best dancer. Oh, it is certainly the best way to gain physical prowess, but there must be more to an art than just technique. A sculptor learns his trade and practices with his tools until he can handle them proficiently. That is his skill. But the perfect craftsman is not necessarily a great artist. It is that something extra outside from the world of sculpting that makes one work stand out from another.

The same is true for dance. When outside influences are blended into the dance they add another dimension to the performance. Since I know personally each dancer in this company, I see how directly relative a performance is to a dancer's real personality. Luke's sincerity and devotion to dance are clear and affable on stage, whereas Becky is not noticed at all; she is afraid and hides. On the whole the more interesting one's personality is in life, the more interest their performance carries..

I was invited to a Christmas class reunion party. Billy Peterson telephoned personally to invite me. "Great!" I told him. "Hey, it will be great to see you!" I lied. I never liked Billy. He had gone through the whole twelve years of Collegiate with me. Throughout those years I had often found myself close pals with boys to whom, years before, I had sworn eternal dislike. But my view of Billy never faltered.

What I disliked most were his pretensions. If you asked him where he got his hair cut, he would answer something like "From Alfred Jordon, the hair designer." "Christ! Jason and I paid two bucks at the corner barbershop!"

"Well, it shows," he would whisper.

Billy never had a pimple, he never had to leave class to piss. In the twelve years I knew him I never once saw him blow his nose. And worse, for twelve years he hardly ever wore the same outfit! He had inexhaustible combinations of jackets and ties.

Whenever his clothes *were* repeated Jason would whisper loudly across the classroom, "Hey, Mr. Ballerina [as he sometimes called me], Billy's wearing that outfit again!" I would reply, "Oh no, not *that* outfit!"

Billy would ignore us, but we delighted in the knowledge that it made him boil. The most irritating thing about Billy was that he was so damned good-looking. He had a smooth face with sculptured cheekbones and dark brown eyes. Even though I despised him, I could never help wishing I looked as good. However, a terrific consolation was the curious fact that he never had a girlfriend. And he wanted one. He tried to the point of pitifulness. For some reason the girls never went for him.

At 11:35 I rang the doorbell to the East Side mansion. Oh yes, the Petersons were wealthy. There was disco music coming from within. I wondered if Jason would be there. I imagined Jason would look all tan and muscular like a highly paid model.

A servant opened the door and took my coat. I followed my ears into the party room. What a large room it was. It must have covered the whole ground floor. I was astonished by the tree in the center of the room, a huge imitation tree wrapped with little blue lights. There was nothing else in the room, only bodies—hundreds of people pressed tightly together. I did not recognize anyone. I stood by the door hoping that someone would recognize me and emerge from the mob. I spotted Billy as he slid through the crowd wearing a white captain's hat. He looked like the handsome owner of a yacht. I plunged into the crowd to avoid him. Straining my eyes against the smoke and the darkness I tried to find someone I might want to see.

Who were all these people? Damn it, Billy! Does he still have to impress us?

I reached the far end of the room where people were dancing. All these strangers were bouncing unrhythmically to the relentless disco beat. "What am I going to do?" I wondered. My eyes were attracted to one couple who, unlike the rest, were dancing together. Their bodies were pressed tightly and they swayed calmly to the music. "Jason!" I shouted with joy.

It was Jason, just as I had imagined him! He did not respond to my cry—I could hardly hear myself over the powerful speakers. I was so glad to see him, but I did not move. I was swept with a sudden desire to get out of there. Like a wave of nausea it came upon me. I longed to see Jason, to talk to him. But who could talk here; who could even see! He seemed content, at ease. It irritated me that he should be so comfortable where I was not.

People pushed by me as if I were invisible. But I felt as visible as a zoo animal in the wrong cage. I radiated misplacement. I saw several more classmates but did not pursue them and was relieved when they passed me by. I backed away from Jason, and pushed toward the door. I was reluctant to go, still I hastened to the exit. Half of me wanted to stay.

The night had made me furious. In the taxi home I cursed everything. I was bitterly disillusioned with Jason, or myself, I didn't know which.

The doc said, "O.K." I may start back today if I like, and I do. Hooray! Of course it will take me a few weeks to get back into performing shape, but they will pass quickly compared to these weeks I have spent limping. If I work hard I can make the last two weeks of the winter season. I am nervous to jump again. When you fall off a horse you must get right back on, but when I fell I could not simply stand and try again. Now I have had time to grow cautious and scared of falling again. I must not be afraid.

I left the doc's office with the good news and marched directly to the theater. It was Monday, the day off. The dressing room was vacant just as it had been on those early morning Jacuzzi sessions. My theater case was intact, nothing stolen. I impatiently grabbed my dirty dance clothes and dressed for a workout. Never in my life did I think I would enjoy wearing a dance belt! This day the jockstrap-like supporter felt wonderful. The familiar discomfort of fitting the legs into fifth position was also satisfying. My whole body felt as if it had been overhauled and finely tuned. Like the scarecrow in *The Wizard of Oz* when arriving in the city of Oz, I felt as if I had been fitted with fresh straw and well-sewn joints.

I wanted to go straight to jumps and *pirouettes*, but I could hear the doctor's southern-accented admonition that I must start slowly. I did the *pirouettes* anyway, and the jumps. I was quickly disappointed. The six weeks of reclining idleness had shifted my center of balance off my feet and onto my derriere. My *pirouettes* were wobbly and jumps tiny. Despite this, I returned home passionately happy again, in both mind and body. I trust the ballet nightmares will end now. I have ten days to get back into performing shape if I want to make the last two weeks of the season.

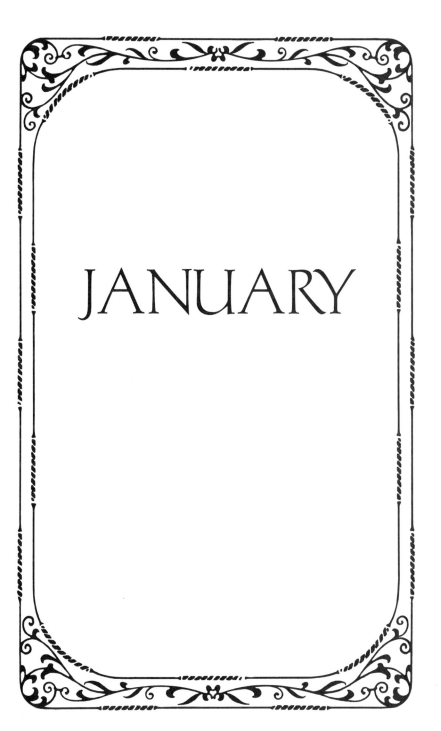

JANUARY

In the Gigue solo of Balanchine's Mozartiana *on the night of the premiere.*

I am a little confused about how to pick up the dancing torch which I dropped with the sprained ankle. To carry it to extreme as I did in my preparation for "Spring" is not only incorrect but detrimental. I intoxicated myself with work. If I continued at that intensified pace, I would burn myself out long before excelling. Where is the middle ground? I am hesitant to begin again without a clear idea of what to do. Shutting out everything and drugging myself with dance will ruin my body and make me crazy again, yet remaining opened to outside interests distracts me from dancing. There must be a compromise where I can function consistently, contentedly, and soberly.

Entering the main studio for a rehearsal was just like coming home after a long vacation. There was the thrill of being back on comfortable ground. There was also a sort of melancholy disappointment because things were just as I had left them.

After a six-week absence I felt like a different person, with a fresh and mature regard for the dance. But everyone seemed exactly the same. Rachael was still telling the same jokes and Gwen was still laughing. Jessica was still cute and being entertained. Why don't they ever change? Do they notice I've changed? Perhaps not. Perhaps volcanic changes from within do not ripple the surface. Or maybe they just don't want to change, like an old person who says, "I don't want anything new, I just want my meals, my cigar, and peace." These are young girls! I don't understand. Perhaps their strongest ambition is to be the same all the time. It's a sort of closed-mindedness. By shunning novelty they render themselves unavailable to anything out of the ordinary. It's so boring. Good God, in New York how far better to be a criminal than to be boring! It's as if they limit themselves to eating salads all the time because they *know* they like salad and would rather stick with something they like just fine than to order something they are unsure of. Imagine a lifetime of salad?

We shouldn't fear anything. Go ahead and order *squid*! If it is *distasteful* to you, then you know it, and the next time someone asks you if you like squid, you can slam your fist on the table and proclaim, "No, I hate it!"

I don't ever want to grow cautious. I don't want to become afraid to take chances. That is a tough thing to do because there is a mighty opponent who seeks to overpower you. He is called RESPONSIBILITY.

Responsibility will whisper in your ear, "Order a salad. If you order squid you might get sick and have to miss a performance."

Damn Responsibility! If I suffer from avoiding it, then it is a fault of mine, but I won't allow it to limit me. I won't have it building walls around me. If, at this age, I am already feeling Responsibility's pressure, will I be able to fight it when it grows stronger?

Please, O mighty God Responsibility, don't weaken me to be cautious, don't make me want to eat salads!

It's wonderful to be able to exhaust yourself. To lethargically shuffle home with tired and worn muscles is a satisfying end to a day—a feeling of accomplishment. I plop into bed and lie staring at the ceiling considering if enough energy remains in me to wash my face and brush my teeth, or maybe I'll just sleep right off.

After a week of classes my body is once again in good shape, only not in the fine condition it was in when I injured myself. Injuries give you a feeling of being set back. As if you have slipped downward on a huge mountain, having almost reached an important plateau. Now you rest below and must climb up again covering already conquered ground. Only this time the ascent promises to be swifter because the path is familiar and the spikes have already been laid.

I rejoined the company with two weeks of performances left in the season. I recalled being alarmed at how quickly I had been excluded from the company when I had hurt myself. Now I was surprised at the uneventfulness of my return. Except for Luke who gave me an energetic "Welcome back," most of the dancers treated me as if I had been there all season. I was simply accepted back into the run of things. No one asked what I had been doing for over a month. The only important thing seemed to be that I could once more carry my share of the work load.

After seven months of performing with the company I had finally begun to feel comfortable on stage. I had grown accustomed to dancing before a pitch-black audience, the bright stage lights were less disorienting, and most of all I had begun to trust myself on stage. It took seven months of performing to feel this; but after six weeks of injury all my experience seemed to have been erased. I waited in the wings during *Suite No. 3* just as terrified as I had been on opening night. I reminded myself that I had danced this several times and that there should be no problem, but after six weeks off stage I was no longer sure of myself.

The performance went well. I didn't make any mistakes, and I did not slip and fall as I had imagined I might. In fact, afterward I was angry that I should have allowed myself to be so frightened about something I knew I could handle.

On a freezing, gray, miserable morning like this only the strongest faith and ambition can pull us from our beds and push us to the theater. We put on the same dance clothes and force our bodies, which are numb from the cold, numb from sleep, into the studio. At ten-thirty we recommence with *pliés*. Mostly the same faces appear each morning, only a handful of company members are consistent in attendance of morning class. Some dancers take class elsewhere; others don't take it at all. Each morning I greet the same faces at the same time. Now the dancers' expressions are worn down, pale, and thinner than at the beginning of this long season. Ironically, they are in their finest shape, yet most pitiful in appearance. They all have the look of a professional marathon runner—gaunt, drawn, yet still able to sprint twenty-six miles. Even though I had just been back performing for a week, the exhausted state of the other dancers was infectious. I too felt that I had been performing for two and a half months.

This morning there was very little conversation. Everyone seemed to be economizing on energy. My body sounded like a bowl of Rice Krispies—"Snap, Crackle, Pop!" Sometimes it feels like trying to tap energy from a cold dead body. This life is just too relentless. Imagine someone offering you the finest of desserts existing; unlimited confectionary displays which are unavailable to the general public. However, they are yours on the condition that you may now devour your fill, but you cannot have any tomorrow or ever again. Dance is an everyday employment for only a short period. It is a quick and excessive career, like over-stuffing on desserts. It may be a wonderful treat, but it's just too much. Too much of a good thing. There is no release, no balance. I can never take a break, a six-month vacation is impossible. Hell, I can't even rest on my one free day a week! Ballet is so exasperating in its demand because it is self-propelled involvement; there is no one to blame but yourself. I don't *have* to work hard. I don't *have* to dance all year long. But for me, the only way to keep this treasure from souring is to stay with it, grow with it, and never leave it. If I left it, I could never come back.

By the time we reached the end of class the fatigued feeling had increased. People did the jumps with effort and delicacy as if dancing with glass feet. John Taras was making an attempt to inspire energy in us. He stood at the head of the room speaking with short energetic breaths. "Jump! And again. That's good! Once more . . ."

There was a sudden "thud" audible over the piano. The whole class seemed to freeze in midair. The music stopped and all heads turned to Caroline. She sat on the floor with her left leg twisted under her right. She made no sound.

We all knew of course. She was injured. Either she had broken her foot or torn ligaments; it really didn't matter what she had done, the point was that she was hurt.

Luke picked her up just as he had done me. In absolute silence he walked out of the studio with her in his arms. The atmosphere of the hushed studio was as if someone had died. We watched her disappear down the hall as we would watch a funeral procession. Then she was gone.

The piano resumed, John continued to pique our energy, and Caroline was no longer thought of. In the back of everyone's mind was the knowledge that she was on her way to the hospital and that she was in pain, but there were other problems at hand. We all turned back to the mirror and concentrated again. Perhaps today we might feel a little stronger, or faster, or a little less tired.

Bette Midler was singing the "Boogie Woogie Bugle Boy" in my ears while I did *jetés* at the barre. I was oblivious to all outside noise because of the high intensity of the Sony Walkman earphones. I finished one side and turned to the other. "He's the boogie woogie bugle boy of Company B . . ." I was now facing the wall where tomorrow's schedule was posted. Suddenly, like a swarm of flies whirling about food, girls came from their dressing room and darted around the schedule. Their left hands held their robes closed, while their right hands were free to punctuate their exclamations. It was amusing to see

Doing barre with the walkman.

their spasmodic movements while hearing only "The company jumps when he plays reveille, He's the boogie woogie . . ." I understood what the commotion was about without overhearing. Mr. B. was going to teach class tomorrow.

After a few minutes the girls left the schedule unattended. I quit the barre to confirm my guess. Sure enough there it was: 11:00—class—Balanchine.

This would be the first time he has taught since I entered the company. I grew instantly nervous. I pushed the rewind button on the tape recorder and rushed back to the barre. I started all over again with *pliés*, like the child who brushes his teeth twenty times just an hour before going to the dentist.

It is curious what a large role confidence plays in dancing. A dancer must be convinced that he is talented and that his dancing has value. Or, if he is not convinced, he must be able to persuade others. Dancers must always leap without looking, step proudly forward and say, "Here I am, and I'm good!" If you are good, then the audience will love it. And if you're not, then often they are still fooled by your belief.

I gave this lecture to myself while gazing in the mirror before class this morning. In twenty minutes Mr. B. would be walking through the door and making us dance. I had arrived an hour before class covered in plastic sweat pants, leg warmers, and a sweat shirt. But now I stood only wearing tights and a shirt. "Damn it, you are going to show him just exactly what you've got!" I prodded myself, but the mirror attempted to dissuade me. I had to admit my leg muscles had developed quite a lot, and the feet did point a little better, but not enough. However, if I beam with great confidence, I might convince even Mr. B. that I am better than I really am.

By eleven o'clock the class was packed. Dancers I had never even seen in company class were present today. At five minutes after, Mr. B. walked in. Everyone's eyes followed his path to the front of the studio. He clapped his hands and the class began.

It's very peculiar—I have done *pliés* consistently now for years, yet just after a few of them in Mr. B.'s class my legs were depleted of strength and crying for mercy. The same was true for *tendus* and *jetés. Oh God, the jetés.* We did so many, so fast that my legs turned to jelly. From there he bypassed everything else and went directly to *adagio* at the barre.

"Just *développé* to the side," he instructed. "Go."

He did not tell us how long we were to hold our legs up. He just walked around the room speaking softly, "Hold . . . hold . . . hold . . . now close fifth, again lift, hold . . ." As he walked about the room everyone, although looking straight forward, was keenly aware of his attention.

There is a story about a giant whose right arm was so powerful he could fell trees with one swoop. He was hopelessly in love with a princess who reciprocated this love, but she was bound to an old and ailing husband. Until the day the husband died she was forced to remain by his side. The giant could not bear to be so near his love yet unable to love her, so he left and roamed the mountains waiting for the day when she would be free to come to him. He walked and walked, and as he walked he would swing his right arm felling a tree with every step, leaving behind a path of fallen trees for his princess to follow when she could. It was a fantastic sight to see, great pine trees toppling in a line one after another as he passed them.

As Mr. B. walked through the studio of dancers with their legs held high into the air the same phenomenon occurred. Each leg in succession would drop to the floor as he passed.

I swore to myself that I would never drop my leg, but alas, I too was defeated. Certainly *all* the dancers did not drop their legs, but the general impression was of trees toppling in the woods.

When we left the barre and moved to the center of the studio, I stood right in front of the boys' group. I felt absolutely naked, yet determined not to hide. For the rest of the class Mr. B. complained that we danced like zombies.

"You know the movie where a man comes out of the grave and goes after the living to eat them?" he said. "You see even the dead get hungry. Now, show me, do you know how a zombie walks? Who knows?" Everyone chuckles except for Luke who was seriously conjuring an image of how a zombie walked.

"Do you know?" Mr. B. asked him. Luke looked straight ahead, his gray eyes were glazed, slowly he raised his arms outward and shuffled forward.

"*Aaaaaaaahhhhhhrrrrrgggg,*" he moaned. "That's right!" Mr. B. yelled. "Good, now you see, zombies are dead people, but you are not dead, you are alive, so show me!"

One thing I could not be accused of was being a zombie. In fact, mine was the opposite fault. I was so energetic, so enthusiastic, that when class was over I felt embarrassed, as well as exhausted. I must have looked like a caricature of enthusiasm. It was too much. I felt foolish; obscene almost. I suppose that anything, even a good thing, taken to excess can become distasteful.

Our union rules state that the dancers must receive a five-minute break from rehearsals every hour. This rule is loosely but adequately followed.

When Rosemary gave us "FIVE" all nine boys scattered off into different directions. Some lit up cigarettes, others

Mr. B. teaching class.

went for sodas, most just sat on the floor to pass the time with light chatter.

We had just finished learning the finale of *Union Jack*—Balanchine's tribute to England. The first section has seven military regiments—thirty males, forty females—all dressed appropriately in kilts complete with sporan and garters. Traditionally, men are not supposed to wear anything under these kilts, but Luke assured me that the ballet was merely a tribute and not authentic. While the second section, which depicts the pearly dancers of the London cabarets, is in progress, we remove our kilts and dress in sailor suits for the last section—the Royal Navy.

I did not know if it was by design or coincidence that I was put in the front of the Scottish regiment of nine boys, directly behind my father. Luke whispered in admonition, "Always keep an eye on your father, he makes mistakes." That puzzled me, for my father was not prone to error. But soon I discovered that the difficulty of remembering the opening steps justified error. In the start of the regiment we have to walk twenty-four counts starting on the right foot. Then we halt and raise the right arm above the head. This is done in severe military manner. No wonder my father made mistakes. The hardest dance steps to remember are those simple basic ones. Every time we repeated the opening I panicked just before commencing. Did we start on the right foot? Did we raise the left arm or the right? "Whatever your father does," Luke continued, "we all have to follow him, 'cause he is in the front and cannot see us."

"What about the sailor section?" I asked. "Do I have to follow him there too?"

"No, he has a solo, and we have our own steps to remember there."

I was reciting "Right foot—twenty-four counts—right arm . . ." when Rosie called the five-minute break. I marched deliberately to the back of the studio and dug T.

Jacques leads the Dress McCloud regiment in Union Jack.

H. White from my leather dance bag. The paperback gets shabby from mingling with the dirty dance clothes. I opened *The Once and Future King* to the folded page and forced concentration on the words. It takes great effort to instantly enter a book. Particularly knowing that there are only a few minutes before another page must be folded and the book again pressed shut. I recalled having left Merlyn lecturing Arthur, but as my eyes perused the words my mind registered "right foot—twenty-four counts—right arm." It takes a good two minutes before I can block out *Union Jack* and listen to Merlyn. Five-minute breaks generally last about seven minutes, so I get a complete five minutes of comprehensive reading . . . "The best thing for being sad is to learn something; that is the one thing that will never fail you." So says Merlyn, but Rosemary says, "O.K., let's learn the sailor section." Back into the bag goes the grimy paperback, and as Rosie demonstrates the steps I intensely observe her, but all I register is "The best thing for being sad is to learn something."

"The best thing for me is to learn these steps," I think to myself and force myself to apply my mind to dance.

This kind of fickleness frustrates me on both ends. But I do manage to assimilate about thirty minutes of reading a day without compromising my dancing, and so far my literary itch is assuaged.

"George is here." Nine kilted boys stood behind my father backstage.

"He's here?" my father asked.

"I think so," I returned. "I talked to Mom on the phone, and she said he had arrived and was on his way to watch the performance."

My father looked far away, as if he had not been listening. "Aren't you excited?" I demanded. After all, the Air Force had kept my brother away for a year now.

"Oh, of course I'm excited, but let's worry about getting through this performance first." There was something troubling my father. Just before the curtain rose he looked back at us questioningly. "We start with the right foot?"

We all paused a second, closed our eyes in concentration, then answered confidently, "Yes, the right."

"Twenty-four counts," Luke reminded him.

My father turned to face the stage and counted down to our entrance "six-five-four-three-two-one-GO."

Out from behind the back wing my father sternly led the nine boys. We marched in three lines behind him. After twenty-four counts all ten men halted simultaneously. My father proudly raised his left arm above his head.

The *left*? I thought it was the right!

"Follow him!" Luke commanded. In tentative sequence nine left arms were raised.

So we began our dance, twisting the kilts around as we skipped through the steps. Every time my father's and my eyes met we beamed grins at each other. We would almost chuckle at the excessive pride we felt for each other and for ourselves.

Off stage afterward, I marked through the finale for memory, when I saw Rosemary walking quickly toward me. She looked so grave and urgent that I guessed I had made a mistake and she was coming to reprimand me. She spoke in a whisper. "How well do you know your father's sailor solo?"

"My father's solo?" I asked dumbly. She nodded.

"Well, I've *seen* it." I did not understand what she was getting at. Behind her my father painfully limped toward me. Now I understood.

"Oh no! *No!* I can't!"

"Yes you can." My father spoke with calm assurance.

"What happened?" I asked.

"I don't know, but my leg won't bend. I can fake it through the finale, but the sailor section is impossible."

"The understudy has left," Rosie put in.

I looked at my father, and he at me. We exchanged glances of urgency. "You walk out for eight counts," he began . . .

After the finale of the first section I dashed to the hall where three dressers were waiting to help me from kilt to sailor suit. They had been warned of the urgency of a swift change. As six hands pulled and twisted the costume my father stood explaining, "Then you do two *pirouettes* and stop on the count of five." I stood dazed. All this was happening to me, but I seemed not to really have a part in it. "Then you hop backward moving your arms like you are rowing a boat . . ." I forced panic away; I could not let my mind cloud. I concentrated solely on my father's instructions. "Then the corps will form two lines; you go between them . . ." I was so concentrated I hardly noticed that his sailor suit was a comfortable fit. In the background I heard the music for the first dance of the sailor section. My father's section was next.

"Then you start the last circle of jumps, and you're finished."

I stood in the wings and watched the eight corps boys run on and salute. I was supposed to be out there, but instead Alex was now saluting in my costume—and I stood shaking, in my father's. As far as my mind was concerned, I was in control. I recited the sequence of the steps aloud.

"What comes after the rowing step?"

"The double *tours*." My father stood behind me reminding me when I got stuck. "You'll be fine," he assured me and rubbed my shoulders. The thought crossed my mind that it really was conceivable that I *would* be fine. I mean I could very possibly pull this off.

"O.K., Chris, get ready, remember walk eight counts."

I felt like a rookie parachuter staring out of the plane at the earth thousands of feet away.

"*Oh my Goooooddd!* . . ." I marched out feeling myself swagger in the manner of my father. It was most peculiar. I had seen him dance these steps and had, in my mind, a mental picture of him. As I executed the same steps I felt just the same as the mental picture. I felt sure that if I could have seen myself, I would have looked just like my father. I swelled with the confidence of my father. I flew through the last circle of jumps and saluted profusely as I skipped backward off stage, just as my father had done. I heard everyone backstage applaud. The other dancers were as relieved as I.

A husky man of twenty-four with a short crew cut and a mouthful of grinning teeth yelled my name after the performance. I turned, recognizing the voice. My brother came forward, and we embraced, squeezing each other. He took a step away from me to look at the sailor suit.

"It *was* you!" He laughed. "I thought so, but I wasn't sure. I kept thinking, 'Yes it is Chris, no it's Dad, or is it Chris?'"

I eagerly told him the story. "By the way," he asked, "where is Dad?" We looked, around the backstage. He was gone.

"He's at the doctors," Rosemary informed us. "Good work, Chris," she said, smiling. I could have hugged her, I felt so excited.

A piece of floating cartilage was the diagnosis for my father's knee trouble.

Within my father's knee there is a piece of cartilage that is broken off and floats around freely. On occasion it might catch in the knee joint, and that stops the knee from bending. There is no way to guarantee that it won't happen again, unless he has the piece removed. By nightfall the piece had released my father's knee, and he was back to normal.

That was a hell of an exciting way to end a season! It

The sailor dance in Union Jack.

was right out of the soap operas—the star hurts himself and an unsuspecting chorus boy gets a shot and succeeds. However, in this case it was a father and son. That performance got me hypercharged with the desire to dance, and instead we have a week's vacation. Next we are scheduled for a short tour of upstate New York.

As I understand it the state of New York gives the company a large grant each year, and there are complaints that since the state gives the money, we should not dance exclusively in New York City. So, in recognition of this complaint, we will be dancing four days in Rochester, a week in Syracuse, and a final week in Buffalo.

Several of the dancers are denouncing this tour with foreboding. They do not wish to visit upstate and are fearful of the conditions we might encounter there. I would not miss it. I am only just beginning to feel really in shape. I would dance on *concrete* without a qualm. The ants in my pants are piquing my legs to dance. I am so excessively charged with desire that there must be a whole colony of ants at work!

FEBRUARY

With Kyra Nichols in Irish Fantasy. *One of Jacques' early chore-ographic successes, he danced the lead role for many years.*

Early this morning the whole company was to meet in front of the stage door at the State Theater. The buses were supposed to leave at 7:30. I was there early. I rested my bag on the marble ledge that surrounds the building, and waited. It was a beautiful morning, cold but crisp and sunny. Such mornings cannot fail to make one feel good. I was content just to be sitting, waiting to go somewhere. I had no decisions to make, I just had to sit and wait to be told what to do.

Two taxis pulled up directly before me. Penny emerged from the first with her luggage. Two huge blond Yves St. Laurent suitcases, and a smaller matching one. I almost expected her clothes to match her luggage—her hair matched! I gave her a hand moving her bags to the curb. She asked if I would watch her things while she went into the theater.

Dennis came out of the second cab. He also had fancy luggage. When I look at Dennis I wonder if he would rather have been a woman. His features are so feminine and fine and he's built curved and petite. He is not a happy person, probably because there was some genetic mix-up. He should have been born a female.

The familiar figure of Rachael caught my eye as she pulled her bags behind her on a baggage cart. She came from the East Side, while another cab pulled in from uptown. Looking downtown I saw two more dancers with two more luggage carts. From everywhere at increasing intervals dancers were heading toward me. Looking down the plaza of the Lincoln Center I could see a parade of turned-out legs and baggage carts. It was eerie. Out of this silent vacant New York City morning suddenly a burst of people converged on one spot. The bags began to pile up—my bag was blanketed by several layers.

Jeremy and Paul came out of another cab. They ran around the place as if it were a party. If it wasn't 7 A.M., they would be drinking beer. By 7:25 practically the whole company was gathered awaiting the arrival of the

179

buses. There was little enthusiasm on most faces. Becky was already complaining. "Where are the buses?" she asked each dancer individually as if the absence was apparent only to her. Very quickly many dancers found themselves little niches in which to sit and wait. No one came to sit with me. Alienation gives the separate party the ability to watch what is going on as a spectator, and to analyze. The outcome is usually laced with a bitter disdain.

All around me the dancers had fallen into their respective cliques. Dennis was surrounded by other males. They sat slouching, dragging on their cigarettes. They were analyzing too. I don't think they really like each other's company and are collectively alienated. They will sit together and criticize everyone else.

Another group is gathered around Rachael and Gwen. They are all laughing. I'll bet Rachael is racking her brain for some joke that will be applicable to this upstate tour.

Constantly mingling among each group is the inseparable carefree party gang. They are always acting as though they are at a party. They flirt with all the girls. Each one of them would take home any of the women who would consent, and just because of this, none of the women consent.

The last recognizable group is the cluster of unpopulars. They don't have a group. Rather than being alone they sit together quietly bored. The universal topic of all these groups is the unpleasantness of this tour. They are constantly finding fault, while I continue complaining about their constant complaints.

It is interesting how differently each person will find a way to make himself feel superior. It's a fault of human nature that we all want to feel we are better than someone else.

Well, here I sit alone. Analyzing everything, feeling superior. I lost my pure feeling of optimism which glowed in me when I first placed my bag on the pavement. Mr. B. says you can practice being happy. Well, I'm determined to be happy on this tour. No matter what.

With that thought I loaded my luggage onto the bus which finally arrived and secured myself a window seat.

Rochester is a very small city, loaded with money. All this money, obviously, has never been invested in their theater. In the larger ballets, the corps would be cramped by the small dimensions of the stage. Advantageously, the hotel was adjacent to the stage door. This allowed me to return me to my room during my frequent one-hour breaks, a luxury I cannot enjoy in New York. There was another luxury here in the hotel lobby, for midway down a dark hallway was a glass door leading to a large circular Jacuzzi. It seated up to ten people, and bubbled perpetually day and night.

Having slept during the bus trip, I found myself alert and awake at three in the morning. I contemplated what I might do. Then I leaped out of bed wrapping a towel around my waist, and descended the stairs into the lobby. I was certain that the hotel did not encourage 3 A.M. skinny dips in their Jacuzzi, so I crawled on my hands and knees under the front desk where the night porter sat, then walked quickly down the hallway. My bare feet on the brown carpet made no sound. My heart's excited pounding was the loudest noise. As I neared the door I heard a faint murmur of music. Fearing that someone might be coming, I dashed forward, flung open the door and slipped safely inside.

"Come on in!" Luke invited. Eight dancers were splashing around, drinking beer and listening to a radio. Luke motioned me to a vacant spot by him. But before I joined them I had to return to my room to fetch a bathing suit, since everyone else had one. We all sat up to our necks in hot swirling water, and stuck our feet up in the center of the tub. Our similar proportions enabled us to form a small circle by touching feet in the center. We laughed at the ugliness of our toes. They looked like little monsters peeking up from the depths of a turbulent ocean.

Around 4 A.M. I began to feel the sandman calling me back to my bed, so I took my leave of the club, wishing a good night individually to each dancer. It sounded like the Waltons.

"Good night, Luke."
"Good night, Chris."
"Good night, Jessica."
"Good night, Chris."
"Good night, Paul."
"Good night, Chris . . ."

The greatest pleasure to be found in Syracuse was our hotel—a grand old building, three blocks from the theater, with high ceilings and hanging chandeliers. My room had a large television and a huge double bed with three pillows. I never watch TV in New York, except when I'm injured or sick, mainly because it terrifies me. I refuse to have one in my apartment even though someone offered me his old Sony. When I am in a room with a TV an immediate battle begins—in which the TV always triumphs. I don't read, write, or do anything constructive. It makes no difference what is on, the tube hypnotizes me, puts me in a trance, drains my energy, gives me a headache. When I finally turn it off, I fall asleep. It is awful to dance after a dose of television—like sleepwalking.

Upon meeting this huge color monster face to face in my hotel room, I acted instantly, rushing toward it before it had a chance to defend itself. I pulled the cable from the wall and pushed the creature into the corner facing the wall. And there it sat screaming for attention. I had won the battle, but alas lost the war, for last night, in a moment of extreme weakness, I reconnected it. I am now doomed until we move into another hotel.

The best thing about this Syracuse hotel is the lobby. In the far corner is a little cluster of heavy chairs and small tables. These are flanked by large plants, and there is a piano. From four to six each evening an old balding man in a red suit quietly plays a medley of forties hits. I am usually finished rehearsing in time to listen to the piano while sipping Earl Grey tea. To my delight, no one else is there. All the seats remain empty, leaving only myself, the pianist, and the waiter. Each day I look forward to the time when I can return to the hotel. Oh what pleasure it is, just to sit when tired, drink when thirsty, and hear soft melodies. It clears the day's tensions and makes all thoughts simple. All the other dancers pass by. Somehow they don't see me. I feel curiously separated from them, like a spectator, totally content in these moments. Oh the joy of simplicity!

This morning when I was on the way to the theater, the light ahead of me was preparing to turn red. I was late and couldn't wait for it to turn green again. I dashed to cross before it changed. I didn't make it. I traveled about three steps before I realized that I could hardly run! My sore back and hips and feet all felt so stiff and arthritic that it hurt to attempt to run. Christ, just a year ago I ran the eight blocks to school to avoid being late to my 8:30 class! Now I am reduced to a pitiful walklike jog that looks like someone with a hangover. I can't believe it, I'm only just nineteen years old!

It's like waking up suddenly realizing that you are no longer a child, things are no longer affairs of fun and games that don't really matter. This is the real thing now! There is no one telling me what to do anymore. I control my life now. I decide what to get up for—or not to get up at all.

If my body hurts it's because I hurt it! My life is in my hands, but I don't know if my hands are qualified for such a responsibility.

Each night when I return to my hotel room I am amazed at the mess I have made with the little material from one suitcase. I keep hoping that the maid will organize my tossed-about clothes and pick up all the papers, but she only makes up the bed. I might clean it myself, but the effort of cleaning greatly outweighs the grief squalor causes. Besides, the disarray will never cause me embarrassment before visitors—I don't have visitors. I have remained sharply separated from my colleagues, my *friends*. I do so because the relationships offered are unsatisfying. In consequence, I am faced with a problem almost worse than the one I discarded—loneliness. I am tormented by it and do not handle it very nobly. However, I would suffer with it rather than return to lesser friendships. It is not pride that keeps me separated but an aspiration for something greater. I seek an ideal friendship.

A frequent cause of failing friendships is an alteration in the things that brought the people together in the first place. My ideal friendship is bound by the pure essential intimate feelings that lie at the heart of each of us. These never change. They are fixed; they are our nature. It is a union deep below the surface so that no peripheral inconstancy affects it. It is as if each rifts his breast, exposing all to the other. Their souls meet. I don't like to use the word "soul" because of the religious implications, but it is the same. One's naked self is a fearfully dangerous thing to reveal. It can only be attempted through immense mutual trust. The spirit in one dies if the other holds back. Like Siamese twins joined at the heart—to safely remove one would leave the other exposed to death.

Physical closeness is a vital part of this *ideal* partnership. Between men and women most physical contact seems to lead directly to sex, and sex is the strongest wrester of unions. The simplest manner in which to evade the potential danger of sex is to avoid sex altogether. So for that reason my ideal friend must be a man.

I do not suggest that I shun women and sex. Of course not. But the problems inherent in sex would render the achievement of the *ideal* friendship with a female increasingly difficult. I could be most free with a man, most comfortable. I want this male partner in addition to a woman.

"I believe in the *additional* perfect relationship between man and man.—Additional to marriage."

"I can never see how they can be the same," said Gerald.

"Not the same—but equally important, equally creative, equally sacred, if you like . . . You've got to admit the unadmitted love of man for man, it makes for a greater freedom for everybody, a greater power of individuality both in men and woman."

D. H. LAWRENCE

We all seek to express the individuality in ourselves, to accentuate those qualities that are unique in us. But our very individuality is dependent on relationship. We are not separate from anything until we can be compared to other things. It follows that the greater the intricacies of comparison, the more room there is for individuality. The deeper one's relationship, the more uniqueness is revealed. Since no two people are alike, the closer and more profound a connection is, the more subtle differences can be recognized, and, in a sense, the farther apart they become.

The objective in this pure relationship is to reveal the deepest thing there is, your core, your uninhibited self, reveal that to one another, and in doing this you have touched where no one else has. All the individuality that is uncovered from this union is dependent totally on the existence of your partner because only he has seen it, and vice versa. In effect, the deepest sense of yourself exists because of your partner's sharing of it.

There are no regulations; no models to imitate. It must be like two people who live on opposite sides of an otherwise deserted island. Each acts totally independent of the other yet they are irrevocably bound because they are together and alone on this island. Two separate individuals, dependents.

But is all this rant possible? Yes and no. I believe it is possible, but I don't think I can ever have it—nor can anyone who might be reading this, because it is too late for us. We grow too scared and unsure to ever be able to trust far enough, or more importantly, to be able to promise our own trustworthiness. But it is possible somewhere in the future when people are not so scared.

As much as I feel the vital need for the one woman in my life, I also feel the need for the male friendship. I would not feel complete without it. I want one of each, and only the best of both.

The writings of D. H. Lawrence lead me to understand this kind of ideal relationship. He knew more about it than I. He died without ever finding it.

Buffalo must be the armpit of New York. It's a shame how quickly one's optimistic feelings of inspiration can vanish. There is no feeling of creativity here. Everything seems gray and dead.

We have a bus in Buffalo. It has been chartered by the company. It leaves the hotel every half hour and delivers the dancers to the door of the decrepit theater. The distance between the hotel and theater is merely six blocks. We are bussed, not because of distance, but for safety. This is a neighborhood of broken windows, dangerous bars, and drunkards. The condition of the theater reflects its neighborhood. Directly across from the entrance is a porno palace. There is no studio in the theater, only the stage for rehearsals. The girls' dressing room is on the sixth floor, the boys' is two flights higher. There is only one elevator and we have been told to take it at our own risk. Sometimes the door does not open, and we are forced to climb the stairs.

I sat in the dressing room awaiting my entrance in the last ballet. There was a half hour left before I would go on. I began to worry about Luke. He had not appeared yet. I was thinking about informing Rosemary when I heard him panting up the stairs. "Boy, are you late," I scolded. "You just have enough time to make up and get in costume. You'll never get to warm up." Luke laughed. "Warm up? You forget this is Buffalo. I don't have to warm up here. All I have to do is climb the damn stairs to the dressing room and I'm all warmed up." He was right. They were an awful eight flights. Climbing made the thighs feel like lead. I sat there and watched while Luke put on his makeup. He looks much better with makeup; we all do. It's not fair that women can wear makeup publicly and men can't. The women complain about not having equal rights; it's the men who are deprived! Men cannot wear makeup; women have a choice. Men cannot wear women's clothes; women have the choice, they can wear either.

Half an hour later, Luke and I stood ready backstage. We were all warm from our flight down the stairs. Luke looked worriedly at me and said, "I don't know about this. After climbing back up those stairs, I may not make it home tonight. I should probably just plan on sleeping there." I looked at him and laughed. Suddenly I felt sorry for him. "Oh no! Luke, I have some really bad news for you."

Luke could see that I was sincere. He feared the worst. "What is it?" he demanded. "Tell me quick."

I told him. "You forgot your hat!"

His hands flew to his head. "Oh no," he whined, "oh no!"

I looked on stage. "You had better hurry up," I warned. "Where is it?"

He looked at me miserably. "It's up in the dressing room!"

He turned, looking defeated, and walked toward the stairs.

I was feeling energetic. I ran past him yelling, "I'll get it." I had to hurry because our entrance was soon. My foot touched the first stair and something caught my eye: the sign on the elevator, *"Ride at your own risk."*

"What the hell," I thought. I pulled on the door. It wouldn't open. Naturally it wouldn't. The elevator was on the floor above. I pushed the button and it came squeaking downward. Quickly I opened the door, stepped inside and pushed the button for the eighth floor. Nothing happened. I pushed the button again. Again nothing. I figured I had better just run up the stairs. I reached for the door handle, but it moved out of reach. I was moving upward. The elevator had decided to give me a lift after all. It wasn't such a rickety machine. Very slowly and noisily it ascended. I held my breath trying to be as light as possible. When it stopped on the eighth floor I forced open the door and ran down the hall into the dressing room. Luke's hat was right on top of the table. I grabbed it and ran back to the elevator. Why not ride since it was already there?

I heard the music approaching for my entrance. Luke would have only enough time to plop on the hat, no time for pinning it. If it fell off, too bad. I flung open the elevator door and stepped in. Well, I almost stepped in. Thank God I didn't.

My right foot, not feeling the elevator floor, sent off a screaming alarm. "Mayday, Mayday." My brain received the message and directly dispatched another message to my arms to grab for anything around. My arms reacted admirably and caught the sides of the doorway, preventing my fall. My hand even clung to the hat.

Having regained my balance and my cool, I looked downward. The elevator rested on the ground floor. I turned and ran down the stairs congratulating my brain for its well-executed safety procedures.

"Ya did good." I complimented my reflexes. That cursed elevator. The door should not have opened without the elevator being there. Well, I shouldn't be surprised. After all, as Luke said, "This is Buffalo."

I was sitting in a restaurant having dinner by myself. I had a book along to read while digesting. As I read, I noticed two of the dancers had come in and taken a table across the room from me. They are two of the worst gossips in the company. They gather gossip and use it to their own ends. Everything is politics to them. They play up to the right people, using little bits of gossip to influence a person's judgment of someone else. They will analyze everyone from the highest to the lowest and figure just how to manipulate them for their own gains. They are dancers. What are they wasting their time on? Why not just dance and enjoy it? Why all this horrible backhanded double-dealing? Why this duplicity? It is all so petty. Yet it runs their lives. It is more important to them than dancing. They desire, like most of us, to become principal dancers, but their motives are spurious. They want to be stars because they want the status, the power, not because they desire to dance better roles. It's like a man running for senator not because he wants the job, but because he wants to be able to say, "I am a senator."

The deeper I get into this world of dance the more I feel as though I am building walls around myself. The more I put into the dance, the higher the walls climb. Like any society, this company has its own do's and don'ts, its own rights and wrongs. And the same abhorrence I feel for the outside society, I also feel for this one. It makes me angry because it renders me intensely conscious of any action I might perform that is out of the ordinary.

Like the feeling you might get upon seeing a wild hat in a store window and instantly adoring it, buying it, and running home with it. However, you can never wear it in public because it's just too outrageous. So the hat sits home in the closet collecting dust. Even if you have the courage to wear the hat, you would always be conscious of the fact that everyone is shocked by it and disapproves. Obloquy would spoil the charm you originally saw in the hat. However, if by some miracle the streets were suddenly vacated and not another person was in the city, you would be happy with your new hat and wear it joyfully without qualm.

It is this kind of influence I abhor. And it exists in any society, even in a ballet company.

From the corner of my eye I saw them looking at me; they were talking about me. I felt like yelling, "Don't talk about me. Don't include me in your games! Do what you wish, but leave me to do my work." They sat there and discussed me, not in the manner that one might talk about someone in whom they are truly interested. They wanted only to figure out how I would fit into their scheme. They wanted to determine how best to use me to their advantage. I hardly know them. We have spoken "hellos and good-byes," but that is the extent of our communication. Yet soon they will be spreading either praise or vilification depending on their predictions of my effect on their motives.

It disgusts me. Yet it is part of this life, part of this closed society in which I wish to participate. I know it would be to my advantage to befriend these people. It would help me in the long run.

All my life I have learned to compromise myself to please people who, in turn, might favor me in the future. I learned the subtle wiles of false flattery. But how I abhor it now. I am disgraced when I think of it. I would never consciously allow it again, but sometimes it comes reflexively. I wish to defy this part of my nature. I must succeed, or I will be forever torn.

In order to continue in this "society within a society" I must learn to function successfully, separately. I must discover a method of being first off and wholeheartedly a dancer. Yet at the same time, not to live the dancer's life. This sounds vague and impossible. It is the same kind of feeling I have for my ideal friend: I know it's there, and understand it. But I don't quite know how to go about finding it.

On the return bus trip I sat alone in the back of the bus taking up two seats. I was rude to the other dancers by hinting that I wished to sit alone. I sulked like a child who didn't have anybody he wanted to play with.

Wait a minute, that's just it! It's just the opposite of what I have been thinking, just the contrary! *I* am the one at fault! I have shunned the friendships and the life in the company, claiming that they are inferior. But it is *I* who am the failure. I am the one who cannot function properly within the society in which all the other dancers thrive. My inability to adapt, my pouting weakness has brought upon this self-exile. Perhaps my "ideal friendship" is merely an excuse, a scapegoat so that I may circumvent admitting failure.

Did I sever these binds because I truly believed them to be unworthy? Or did I not receive enough attention and therefore threw them away as a child might toss aground a toy he is unable to operate. The child inculpates the faulty mechanism of the toy, yet another child retrieves the discarded toy and contently and successfully manipulates it. Am I the child who kicks up the game board rather than lose the game?

I don't know, perhaps.

I've got to stop all this figuring out of how I want to live my life. I waste all my time searching for the *way* to live. I analyze so much that it becomes no longer living but reciting, acting. I live as if followed by a hidden camera; each breath is observed and regulated. I cannot sneeze without analyzing and determining if I really wanted to sneeze and how I wanted to sneeze in the future—hours of cogitation over the ideal sneeze. What the hell is the ideal sneeze!

It is because my mind is unpredictable and constantly shifting that I feel uneasy. I always feel the need to know just what I'm doing.

Growing up consists of a sort of traveling, a trip from one phase to another. I keep worrying about where I'm going instead of just enjoying the trip. Damn it, I have to stop all this agonizing over "how to" and just "be." Oh what a relief that will be; I'm so tired of making fatal decisions every day.

These are all good people here in the company. My comrades, they are all extraordinary. Instead of forsaking their affability, I should welcome it for nothing more than it is. They are special in themselves. So what if it is not an "ideal friendship." If I abjured all that was less than my abstract ideal, then I would die of starvation—refusing to eat hamburger because it is not mignon.

MARCH

In Gershwin Concerto.

After spending time away from home, returning to the New York City life-style can be a shock to the system.

Having grown up in the city, I have been subjected to a curious sort of influence. There is a little New York insect that lives in the back of my head. He says only a few words: "Go, faster! Do this! Do that! DON'T WASTE TIME!"

A dancer's life is most certainly a harder and more productive one than average, yet nonetheless that little insect complains on my one day off, "You didn't do enough with your free time!"

It is the New York fashion, the city philosophy, that one must always be achieving, always productive, and there are so many things to do in the city it can become quite a burden! One is continually hearing about exciting and interesting things to do.

Everything one does in New York, by law, must be exciting and interesting. But when the free time finally arrives I rack my brain and swear I cannot think of one thing. That's because there is not *one*, there are *thousands*, and they are all registered in my mind under the title of "EXCITING AND INTERESTING." One by one I slip these FARES into my head, like quarters into a machine. But then they all seem to blend together, forming one unit, one mass. This renders it impossible to recall any one separately. I twist with guilt when I hear of something fun to do. I know I'll probably never do it because I realize that this new idea is already becoming part of the mass of coalescent FARES.

We are so buried in interest and excitement that we often fail to see the fault in it: We have no time to simply sit back and appreciate what we have done. We accomplish so rapidly, so relentlessly, that it becomes like running from one meal to another without ever truly enjoying the food.

When the bus entered the city I felt an urgent sort of uneasiness. I was excited to be home but at the same time tentative.

When I was a child I used to play jump rope with my friends. One of the games was called Double Dutch. Two people would swing two ropes while a third person stood on the outside preparing to jump into the middle. One has to time the jump perfectly or you get hit with the rope.

I used to wait so long before leaping in under the rope. I knew that the minute I started, there was no stopping. I would have to keep jumping to stay alive in the game. It always made me feel a little uneasy in my stomach, but once I jumped in there and started hopping, I forgot about all the queasiness.

How my father still dances is beyond me. His floating cartilage has left him alone so he can work once more. Within the past five years he has had cartilage operations on both knees, he has torn the muscle from his arm, and his feet are webbed! Yet, every morning he is there in company class, and he still does his best to jump higher than anyone else.

I don't think there are many people who, suffering all my father's hardships, would still be dancing. I don't think I would. The most impressive aspect of his endurance is that when he performs he really is great. I admire his strength and am glad to see him each morning. We work hard together, and laugh even harder. Admittedly, most of our conversation deals with *les femmes*, which is a topic that never fails to inspire.

Why is it that when a young boy has plenary interest in the opposite sex it is considered "healthy" and is smiled upon with approbation, but this same engrossment fifty years later is scorned?

Why is a young boy "healthy" and an old man "dirty"? I want to know because when the times comes, I don't want to be disdained as a dirty old man!

During that interminable period of my injury, despite the fact that I was prevented from dancing, I found moments of great contentment and exhilaration—a happiness no less intense than that derived from daily dancing. Although I was missing dancing, I was not miserable without it. Perhaps the fact that I knew I should be shortly returning calmed my apprehension.

I could never willingly give up dancing, but I realize now that if fate parted me from it, my life would not be totally destroyed.

There are only two things which I could not live without: music and women. Without both of these life would not be bearable.

Without music I believe I would go mad. I don't pass a day without some sort of exposure to music. I constantly sing to myself down the hallways or the streets. People think I must be happy to be singing all the time, but the reverse is true. It is the singing that makes me happy.

As to women, well, without them that would be it. I would surely lose my mind, if I didn't kill myself first. Sometimes I realize that almost everything I do is indirectly for women. For the more a man has, the more he can offer to women.

During a performance of the *Brahms-Schoenberg Quartet*, while awaiting my entrance I always watch the third movement. There is a short variation for the man. I wait anxiously for its arrival because of the music. Oh, I could almost die to hear it. Suddenly, out of a quiet lead up, the French horns sound the melody powerfully. Immediately, an electric shock goes through me. I feel a surge of energy and strength, courage even, for this is glorious music. I cannot help imagining Laurence Olivier atop a stallion in full battle attire, galloping triumphantly back to his castle followed by thousands of soldiers. I don't know the steps to the variation, but I jump around backstage doing any step. I must jump or I would scream!

I could never dance that variation on stage. I don't think I could contain myself from yelling with glee. This music transforms me instantly.

No wonder this profession is so entrancing. Look at what Mr. B. has done. He has taken the two vital things in life, music and women, and combined them in extraordinary proportion—the best of music and the finest of women. This is truly a man I admire.

Sharing the same theater with me is a man who knows so much about the two most vital things in life and I hardly speak to him. What am I waiting for? Will I wait until he dies and then exclaim, "Oh, if only I could have asked Mr. B."

With this thought I went straight to seek out Mr. B. There was still time before I had to make my entrance. I found him sitting by himself on the other side of the stage. Without hesitation I approached him.

"Mr. B.," I began, suddenly panicking. What did I want to say? He was listening so I had to continue.

"I was wondering if, when you have a little free time, I might talk to you about . . ." I could see in his eyes that was thinking, "Oh, he wants to talk about his career . . ." His anticipation of my question made my actual words surprise him.

"About women!" I finished.

He looked confused.

"What?" he asked.

"Women!" I repeated. Now he understood.

"Naturally!" He smiled. "Very important. Not many man loves women anymore."

The third movement was ending and I had to rush back to the other side of the stage or risk missing my entrance. I told him so and turned to go.

"Naturally," I heard him say behind me.

We are taught from a very early age to be fair. Fairness is a virtue and the good guys really do win. We are also shown at the same time that the practice of justice and fairness are not always advantageous. The boy who studies the hardest for an exam is not necessarily the one who gets the highest grade. The amount of time spent in preparation is not important. The performance is the real test. It is the exam that decides the superior. There is no Olympic medal given to the one who tried the hardest.

The same is true in the ballet. No one asks for a list of the hours you spent working each week. No one cares. It's what you deliver on stage that counts, and by that alone you excel.

In NYCB Balanchine makes all the decisions about who dances his ballets, and Robbins does the same for his. So, consequently, all the dancers' careers are absolutely subject to the whims and tastes of these two men. We answer directly to their likes and dislikes.

Contrary to school, where mistakes are pointed out so that repetition can be avoided, a dancer often has no idea why he or she is not excelling. They must simply assume that something they do, or fail to do, makes another person better for the part; more desirable to the ballet masters.

Today I found out that Luke was not cast for any performances of *Episodes.* I was crushed. That was his only solo role and he was fascinating in it. Before I joined the company Luke had gone through a terribly painful relationship with a woman. Luke's sense of pride is very strong, and this romance crushed him and he almost quit dancing. He got heavy and drank much more than his body could handle. These last six months I have watched him pull himself together courageously, and now he is in the finest shape of his life.

No one told him about the loss of the role, it just went up on the casting sheet that someone else would be dancing it. He was offered no explanation. I wanted to talk about it, but he would not. He just walked away mumbling, "Well, you know how it is."

Our language is inadequate. I find that I have abused the word "great," so that when something comes along truly worthy of laudation I am frustrated to find a way to hail it.

"He is a great artist" . . . "a great person" . . . "a great meal."

The word means so little to me now that it is not enough to describe last night. It was more great than all the things I have called great in the past. It was a combination of extraordinary people:

Suzanne Farrell, Jacques d'Amboise, Lamar Alsop, the concert master, Tchaikovsky, and Balanchine. *Meditation.*

I was worried about my father. He hasn't been able to kneel well for a year. He has pulled his right biceps completely off the bone, and his left shoulder gives out when he lifts. Suzanne has problems also. She had torn ligaments that have not yet healed.

I knew of all their ailments and doubted their ability to pull off the ballet. Like football players they were both taped and wrapped up under their costumes. And so the performance began. Not a pair of eyes in the audience could have guessed that anything was amiss. These were two professionals.

It is natural for a dancer to watch a performance with an eye for the mechanics of the steps. One tends to study how the man partners the girl, or if the girl holds a successful balance. This analytical method of viewing can hardly be avoided by a dancer. However, during this performance, mechanics never crossed my mind. I was totally enrapt. This performance was so powerful and convincing that I was pulled in completely. When it was over I was crying. Really crying—from deep down.

I certainly have cried a lot since joining the company. The last place I wanted to be seen crying was on stage. But the tears just came out, like a big sigh.

Three moments of Meditation. *Choreography by Balanchine.*
Music by Tchaikovsky.

The ballet shows two passionate lovers who, for some uncontrollable reason—some fact of fate or human nature—can never remain together. They are always destined to failure. She leaves him, as she found him, all alone, unhappy, in darkness. Oh, it is indeed very corny, pure romanticism, and wonderful.

After the ballet, I had to leave the stage. I felt embarrassed to be seen. I didn't look up from the floor as I made my way to the cellar. As I passed by the other dancers, I heard their singsong voices: "It was so beautiful!" "Oh, Suzanne was so beautiful!" "Wasn't the music beautiful?" They did not understand, these dancers. They had seen nothing, felt nothing.

I knew that a few other dancers were affected as profoundly as I was, but I would not encounter them for they, like myself, were plowing blindly through the crowds to find a place to be alone. I hurried to my spot in the cellar. I did not cry anymore, I just thought about what I had seen. The combination of these five people had created something greater than any love poem, any painting, any novel. More moving than any artwork in existence. This was the greatest moment of romance I have ever witnessed.

It was strange to sit there, in the cellar, moved by something that no longer existed. The dance lives only in the present. Unlike a book or a painting, I can never again see what it was that moved me so. It does not exist anymore. Only its memory exists. Certainly the ballet may be performed again next week, but it cannot be the same. The music remains the same, the choreography is fixed, but the people who bring those things to life will be different and I, watching it, will be different. These inconstant things make it impossible to repeat. That is the charm of live theater. Often I will read a book and adore it, deriving great pleasure from it and carrying the memory of its treasure. But later I might reread it only to find it uninteresting and disappointing. Then the book loses its original charm. The memory of its joys is destroyed. This cannot happen to the dance. Last night's performance can never be destroyed by future viewing. It is forever fixed in sweet memory.

It was a humbling realization that most people are as insecure—or more so—as I. I never considered anyone as uncertain and sensitive to inadequacy as myself.

In joining the company I learned that general insecurities are quickly tempered when one is first touched by responsibility and the need to make decisions. This dilutes insecurity and one gains control of it. With this heightened awareness, how easily one can spy it in others, in their eyes, their words, actions, or even lack of action.

I felt ambivalent toward this discovery, because on the one side I am relieved and strengthened by being a minority of a majority—like living in a world afflicted by plague and myself apparently having a lesser contamination. On the other side, the pitifulness of all men is shown. I am swept with a strong disillusionment as to my general admiration of mankind.

I am relieved that my insecurity is less than most people's, but I feel no pride, for it's like becoming a principal dancer not because one is so good but because everyone else is so bad.

Tonight was the first occurrence of what I am sure is a rare phenomenon. Having only encountered it this once, and having seen it revealed on the faces of but a few other dancers, I realize its rarity.

Tonight was the performance of *Fancy Free*, the ballet that I sprained my ankle for. Months of work and anxiety would now reveal their value. All past effort was now united into one forceable discharge.

From the second I cartwheeled out onto the stage, I

In Fancy Free.

In Fancy Free. *My "pickup" is Stephanie Saland.*

felt like a giant—a huge man of infinite power and strength, a strength in the control of my own body, an elation of strength. The total scope of life seemed wrapped in the present. It felt as if I controlled the music, as if my dancing made the music play.

Creation, utilizing the utmost of physical and mental concentration, is the secret of what people call "living the moment." For the whole forty minutes of *Fancy Free* I reaped the moment.

The wings were filled with other dancers standing there watching. Mr. B. and Jerry were there too—I noticed this just before the curtain went up. I never noticed them again.

I have heard people try to describe the feeling of

dancing, and it usually ends up sounding religious or mystic. One finds oneself unintentionally using phrases like "another world," or "the ultimate experience." The more sincere the attempt to explain, the more apparent is its ineffability. We do not have the proper words for it. It is as if all the senses were fulfilled, and all desires realized. All fears and disappointments disappear, or rather they are blanketed by the overwhelming force of the positive. It is similar to the exhilaration of winning a race.

The bows finished, everyone headed for the dressing room. I was exhausted, soaking with sweat. Yet I wanted badly to continue. I could not just stop dancing for the night. "Let's do it again." There was such energy in me that I might have burst from it. My whole body wanted to scream out. I could feel my blood pumping.

The stagehands had removed the set and were turning out the lights. Reluctantly, I left the stage for the dressing room. The dresser was annoyed at my lateness. He wanted to get home, and couldn't go until he had put away my costume. I apologized. Although he scolded me, in his heart I believe he liked me and could never be truly angry.

The dressing room was empty. Often I had found it so when I was the first to enter it in the morning. But never before had I been the last to leave. Tonight everyone had changed quickly and gone out on the town because tomorrow was the day off.

Upon leaving, with my bag hanging from my shoulder and a scarf wrapped against the cold, I turned out all the makeup lights and shut the door behind me. In the elevator, on a whim, I pressed the button for the stage level rather than the street.

The backstage was deserted and dark. Placed out in the middle of the stage was the 200-watt light bulb that glared from its metal stand. There was no other light. My boots echoed hollowly as I walked across the stage. I stopped on center stage and gazed outward. The curtain was again raised. Red exit signs were the only lights in the audience. I stood there for quite some time just looking out at the empty theater. It was so quiet that any movement was audible. Something kept racing through my head. A thought. The more I ignored it, with greater intensity did it persist. Then it cried out from my head, and I yelled aloud almost laughing, "I love this life!" This is where I belong, on the stage. I have been standing on it for so long and not even seeing it, not realizing that all the time I was in my element. There are no fears or apprehensions; no loneliness! I was not wanting anything, content, happy.

For the first time there was no longer a shade of doubt. I had landed myself in the right place. Remembering my pledge to wait an entire year before even considering the question of happiness, I knew now that I need not await the completion of the year. This night's performance alone, this one evening of rapture made everything worthwhile—all of it. If I were only to experience this feeling once a year, that would be sufficient. There is such greatness within this specialized world of which I am thankful and lucky to be a part. Here one can experience the greatest high on earth. And this great stage was my home.

How proud I felt standing there looking at the empty theater—so damn proud. Every inch of this world made me swell with lordly affection. The stage, the rosin box, the dressing rooms, all the dancers, teachers, Balanchine, Robbins, the orchestra, all of it—how wonderful it truly is. Dancing is what makes me special.

We are all special here, and *only* here are we special. Pride and overwhelming happiness filled me on that empty stage in the darkness. Then suddenly there was a noise, a door slamming or an object dropped, perhaps. Whatever it was startled me. I searched, straining against the dark, for the origin of the disturbance. Curiously, I felt embarrassed—embarrassed that perhaps someone might have been watching me exuding such emotion. Here I was standing on the same spot where an hour before I poured myself out for thousands to watch. Now I was ashamed that one person might have witnessed me.

It was silent once more. No one was there. Somehow this silence was disquieting—a screaming silence. It was not right to be there. It felt uncomfortable on the stage without lights, without other dancers, without an audience. I quietly hoisted my bag over the other shoulder and walked briskly out.